THE SOUND OF A SUFFERING LAND

PHAN NHAT NAM
Translated from the Vietnamese by
KIM VU

PHAN NHAT NAM

THE SOUND OF A SUFFERING LAND

Translated from the Vietnamese by
KIM VU

SONG PUBLISHING
2025

Dedicated to:

The People of the sacred country of Vietnam

The Devoted Soldiers
of the Army of the Republic of Vietnam

The Prisoners of War in the
1960-1975 War

Copyright © 2025 Phan Nhat Nam
Translation Copyright © 2025 Phat Manh Vu
All rights reserved.

Library of Congress Control Number: 2025907102

ISBN: 979-8-3492-6611-9

TABLE OF CONTENTS

Introduction   7

Story 1: "A Soldier's Day"
         or "The Dead at Christ's Feet"   15
Story 2: "On the silent battlefield"
         or "Communist Cadre, Who Are You?"   29
Story 3: "The Kaolo Pen"   34
Story 4: "The women at Camp 5 Lam Son"   40
Story 5: "Surviving in the Land of Death"   53
Story 6: The Boy Died on the River of his Homeland   57
Story 7: "Two Soldiers" or "After the Conflict"   64
Story 8: "The Rivers Ran through the Rocky Hinterland"   83

About the Author   141
About the Translator   143

Introduction

Phan Nhat Nam was born on September 8, 1943, altered to December 28, 1942. The place of origins was Nai Cuu, Trieu Phong, Quang Tri; The place of birth was Phu Cat, Hue-Thua Thien. Joined the army for the first time on November 11, 1960; for the second time on November 23, 1961. Graduated from Class 18 of Da Lat National Military Academy on November 23, 1963, with the rank of Second Lieutenant. Volunteered for the Parachute Infantry, Battalion 7, Bien Hoa, KBC 4919. Last unit, Military Joint Committee 4 & 2, until April 29th, 1975. After 1975, imprisoned in re-education camps in the North and the South for 14 years (1975-1989), most of which (1976-1988) were in solitary confinement in the prisons of forced labor. Received the death penalty yet not executed. Been incarcerated throughout the Northern prison system, with two periods of maximum security (February 1979 to August 1980; September 1981 to May 1988). Settled in the US at the end of 1993.

A writer for more than fifty years (1968-2023), with the same authenticity and honesty that have been shown in books published before 1975 in Saigon: - *Dau Binh Lua* (1969), *Doc Duong So.1* (1970), *Ai Tran Gian* (1970) - Fictionalization of human beings, stories of political and military events in Hue, Da Nang, Central Vietnam (1960, 63, 66). *Dua Lung Noi Chet* (1971) The Mau Than Spring Tragedy (1968) in Hue, recreated as the novel *Mua He Do Lua* (1972), the Summer Epic of the Army and People of the South in the battle to keep the land and protect the people. *Tu Binh va Hoa Binh* (1974) - An urgent warning after the "disguised Peace" from the fraudulent Agreement signed in Paris on January 27, 1973.

Arrived in America at the end of 1993. Continued writing after the forced interruption since 1975, personally going to readers around the world, across 40,000 miles East-West, Southern-Northern Hemisphere, around the world. The Soldier-Writer must go forward and carry out the work: Reconstructing the true portrait of the People-Soldiers of the country called the ARVN with: *Nhung Chuyen Can Duoc Ke Lai* (1995), *Duong Truong Xa Xam* (1995), *Dem Tan That Thanh* (1997) - Poems written in the endless darkness during the period 1975-1993, in the prison camps of Long Giao and Long Khanh; Hoang Lien Son, Thanh Hoa, designated place of residence after returning from prison in Lai Thieu, Binh Duong, the South; *Nhung Cot Tru Chong Giu Que Huong* - Character Memoirs of People who have devoted themselves to fighting for Justice for half a century throughout the homeland; *Mua Dong Giu Lua* (1997) - Notes after three years in America to remind myself, friends, and successive generations to always keep the faith. *Giu Lua Chien Dau Mua He* (1972), *Chuyen Doc Duong* (2007) (Part I), recounting the stories heard, seen, and lived along with the tragedies of every Vietnamese person in their homeland, around the world, and in America after 1975; *Phan Nguoi Van Nuoc*: Song Publishing House (2013) - Report on the fate of each Vietnamese and the entire Nation that had to bear the burden and suffer exile throughout the war (1945-1975), after 1975; *Chuyen Doc Duong* (Completed) Version: Song Publishing

House (2013).

Books that have been translated: *The Stories Must Be Told:* Friends Translators Group (2002). *A VietNam War Epilogue:* Friends Translators Group (2013). *Stigmates de Guerre:* Translator Phan Van Quan and group of friends, NXSong, US (2015) *Red Summer/L'été Embrasé*: -Translated by Lieu Truong, Harmattan Publishing House, Paris, France (2018). *Peace and Prisoners of War*: Resistance Publishing House (1987) *Peace and Prisoners of War*: Naval Institute Press, US. (2021).

Always "Learn-Read-Write" from the age of 20, 30...or now, 60, 70, 80, whatever the circumstances and conditions - *To talk to the end about Suffering as Karma* - of every human being that has lived with, met, witnessed, heard about in the land called the Indochina Peninsula, with Vietnamese scattered all over the world for more than half a century. It is because of *"Bat Binh Tac Minh"* (the need to cry out as witness to injustices) that necessitated the writing, and not due to talent and style acquired in the intellectual or academic world. Maintaining the spirit of a *"Soldier-Writer"* and not as a professional writer or poet.

With the responsibility of a soldier, protecting the nation; The writer's responsibility is to society, so the *"Soldier-Writer"* always reiterates the ideas and words expressed from the first time he took up writing (1968), still retaining the same value. In 1969, he wrote in *"Dau Binh Lua"*: *"At this age (26 years old), of course I have no more hope in literature, nor do I dream of earning a little fame through the path of literature". Furthermore, the reputation of a writer in Vietnam is not very bright. But (I) still want to resort to writing as a "need".... After eight years in the army (1961-1968), comfortable times are rare, while troubles, having a cause or not, explicit or concealed, seem to be waiting to rise like a storm when opportunities present themselves!*

It is because of these diverse scenes of life that I had to write... Eight years, a time almost equal to the life span of the farmer Johann Moritz (character in The 25th Hour by C.V. Gheorghiu), wandering through the prison camps of bloody Europe... But before and after those eight years, the Romanian man still had happy and hopeful days. What joy do I have in these eight years and what hope do I nurture for a post-war Vietnam!? (Not to mention the total collapse of South Vietnam on April 30, 1975)".

Coming to America at the end of 1993, I still continued to write (the only difference is that in the past I wrote with a pen, and now with a computer). But my situation was no different from that of the young man who just turned 20 thirty years ago. The difference is that I'm now older and can absorb pain better... This was my mood when writing *Chuyen Doc Duong* (2005): "*It took me quite a long time to finish a relatively thin book, and sometimes I felt it was too difficult, making me think I would not be able to finish it. But now I'm done with the writing, with the same sentiment as when I was young when I finished writing Dau Binh Lua (1968-69) - It turns out I used the words truthfully but in reality it didn't get anywhere! Just thinking about that makes me feel exhausted. The social regime (called the Socialist Republic of Vietnam) continued to "**institutionalize, politicize, and rationalize**" the cruelty of life into policy - A typical example of an advanced civilization: the "socialist society". How can we save Man? Where to start in Vietnam? Moreover, today's situation seems to be even more "scary" than during those years long ago. Because in just the blink of an eye, the writer has now become an old man in his sixties - The situation of an old person fallen into ruin, his country lost, his home destroyed! In the past, Du Phu wrote a meaningful poem: "The country destroyed, yet* *the mountains and rivers remain. In spring, the grass still grows gloriously..."* But those are just words and poems to comfort, because in the homeland today, more than forty years after 1975, the trees and people in the fields are dry and miserable to the point of sadness..."

No guns or bullets can solve the suffering over the past half century that I have witnessed and lived through. That's not to say that guns and bullets themselves (weapons of war) have also largely participated in the breakdown of civil society in my homeland Vietnam as well as in the whole world - Therefore, writing is necessary for personal life (material and spiritual) in a specific way. Without writing, how else to live? Even though I (also) understand very clearly: *"In the end words will get nowhere!"* Phan Sao Nam once found out: *"To establish oneself, literature is the worst way!"*

The Vietnam War was one filled with doubts and concerns for many people and for myself. So the question (*to ask myself*) is: *Do you really have absolute confidence in the choice to fight with a gun (yours and your brothers-in-arms of the same generation)?* To answer this question, we must refer to a situation that I myself was placed in one day in June 1972 when the great Southern army under the command of Lieutenant General Ngo Quang Truong launched Operation Loi Phong (June 25, 1972), starting the operation to recapture Quang Tri... *"At that time, when the Summer of 1972 just began, the third month from the day the North Army launched a major attack on the South, Quang Tri and Thua Thien were the first two places that suffered the devastating disaster of heavy bombs and bullets, and the people from these sorrowful places once again carried their children in their arms and their elderly parents on their backs down Road No. 1. The last resort - the Soldier...* **Republican Soldiers, save us people, Republican soldiers!** *On the road covered with dried blood,* *corpses were scattered, the southern part of Quang Tri, in Hai Lang District, all the way to My Chanh Bridge... It wasn't just a few people, but the entire mass of people who called out at the same time like that. When they breathed their last breaths, their mouths wide open, their eyes in stark dismay. They called out to the Soldier as they fell down, their blood flowing from their mangled and bruised body, their hands holding the rosary of the Cross or the Bodhi beads while above their heads, the Northern Army artillery exploded continuously. Cruel explosion... The explosives did not spare a single part of the ground, hitting human bodies. In that desperate situation, the people had only "one hope of rescue" to call on after their religious protection and prayers were trampled by the Northern invaders pretending to be "liberators". Cruelly and contemptuously...* **Republican soldiers**! *People cried out like that more than once. People often cry out like that when facing death, when dying.*

Yes! I have heard my compatriots cry out like that during Mau Than in Hue, 1968; The people cried out, *"Republican soldiers, save the people!"* when running from the battle in An Loc, 1972... People cried for help to Republican soldiers when evacuating from the Central Highlands to Tuy Hoa, Binh Dinh, Nha Trang, March 1975. And after 1975, on the Eastern Sea, on the way to cross the border to get out of the country, all the Vietnamese people (regardless of North/South) became a kind of untouchables, exiled throughout Southeast Asia's refugee camps, in Hong Kong, facing pirates and Khmer Rouge soldiers. And now in the Eastern Sea, facing "unrecognized ships". The Vietnamese people were despised and damned because of one simple thing: **The Vietnamese people no longer had soldiers to protect them** - the Army of the Republic of Vietnam had been shattered together with the Vietnamese Hope. I always firmly believe in **The Just Cause** of the Southern Soldiers despite the defeat on April 30, 1975. The disaster from the dark destiny for the entire Vietnamese Nation was not because the ARVN Soldiers were not good fighters.

Returning to the issue I once wrote about in *"Dua Lung Noi Chet"*, what has *"Death"* (real, always encountered and suffered directly) taught me? So if we have to fall into the situation of *"Dua Lung Noi Chet"*, each person must find a way to save himself, no one can show that to anyone else. On September 7, 1981, when the second period of confinement began, entering the maximum security cell two meters long, three meters high, and one meter wide, life could only be found through the 30x20 cm rectangular vent with an iron mesh above. The temperature in the room was 40 degrees in the summer, and the cell was dimly cold in the winter because the prison was located in the limestone mountains of Thanh Hoa Province. If flies or mosquitoes flew in, they'd land hard because the pressure in the room was too high! The prisoner sat motionless on a mat, his ankles clamped to a U-shaped iron shackle. He defecated and urinated into a bamboo tube; two cups of hard corn, (the kind used to feed animals), and two cups of cold water a day! Sitting in the dark, gradually losing all senses and thoughts in the years 1982, 83, 84... The head sometimes seemed to be in smoke, or boiling in the fire due to sadness and anxiety... How could one survive?! How could every second pass? Yes, every second, not every minute, or every hour! But gradually it passed like the words called POETRY written on the tip of my fingers.. *"Truly I cannot survive. One hour even, let alone a year... Not one year but ten. Endless suffering and pain... But people can Live because there is Heaven!"* Yes, there is Man because there is Heaven!

Later, I was further confirmed that there were other people in similar situations with even more hardships: Captain

Nguyen Huu Luyen spent more than 21 years in prison; Nguyen Chi Thien, 27 years; After 1975, in the 21st century, there were men like Nguyen Huu Cau serving 35 years, and Priest Nguyen Van Ly exceeding 30 years in prison! Those living overseas who *"accused"* Nguyen Chi Thien for being fake and plagiarizing poetry, and did the same for Father Nguyen Van Ly, calling him the *"Dollar prophet"*, were those who have lost "Human Love" - *The animals that rejoice in the suffering of their fellow human beings* - Those who have never known the weight of the shackles, when every second seemed unmoving in the dark cave! Who can I tell this to about each hour and minute on this border of life and death for the time period of 7, 8, 10, 20... years?!

There is a passage in *"Dau Binh Lua"* that can be repeated today after more than 50 years: *"I have accepted my participation in the war, in the hope that my participation would end the war. Winning or losing does not matter, but the important thing is "Don't stay on the sideline, don't run away while your friends and peers are participating and dying. It doesn't matter if you die on this side or that side, dying in hatred or dying by accident..." These lines (that couldn't be more honest) had been written 50 years ago. That year I was twenty-six years old, the Red Summer of 1972 had not yet happened; the collapse of the South on April 30, 1975 had not yet occurred; I had not yet crossed the border; I had not yet assimilated the dark dungeons of concentration camps; 25 times moving residence after 30 years in America! What more can I say about "happiness" and "hope" now?*

February, 2018,
50 years after the Mau Than Hue Event (1968-2018)
Revised August 8, 2023

Story 1

"A Soldier's Day"
or
"The Dead at Christ's Feet"

The Tien Giang River was as vast as the ocean. A large ferry was loaded with three GMC trucks and a few private cars, carrying us across the river along with a group of passengers in colorful clothes. They huddled to one side, watching the soldiers from afar. I sat on the hood of the ferry, dropping pieces of paper into the water, my mind drifting like waves.

The convoy left Highway 4 and turned to the right along the earth road towards Truc Giang airport. Past the district elementary school, coffins were placed in a row; the smell of corpses was overwhelming. Rangers. 41st Battalion. It seemed that the battalion commander or his deputy had died. The soldiers on the trucks were chatting in a casual way. They did not know that the battle was coming to a fierce end, so the Airborne Task Force had added our battalion to another friendly one that had been present in the operation area since the day before. Arriving at the airport where the headquarters of the Tien Giang tactical zone's operational center was located, we were ordered to spend the night here in wait for the helicopters to be transported to the operation area tomorrow. I had not been to any big battle, having no idea of the upcoming difficulty, so I calmly spent a quiet night with the conclusion: A helicopter assault for a parachutist is just a joke–*a piece of cake*.

On the twenty second, at 8 o'clock, two artillery batteries located at the airfield directed their guns towards the landing zone and fired continuously to clear the area. Assuring the enemy's death to secure your own, the cruel law of war. As soon as the gunfire cleared the field, thirty helicopters ascended at the same time and brought the 71st and 72nd companies to the battlefield.

Reported good landing down on the ground. The rest of the battalion was transported by helicopters next. The entire battalion was already down, with the two companies of 71 and 73 leading the battalion, moving along for fifteen minutes. Gunfire! Hit! Touched... The soldiers roamed around, transmitters were sending orders in a flurry. In front of the battalion, the gunfire was mixed. Our sound was dry and hard, the enemy's sharp and pointed... 72nd Company withdrew and moved to the right side of 73rd Company. The order was for our company to move up quickly. As we passed the battalion major's position, a huge explosion flashed right in front of him. The 57mm bullet exploded the instant it came out of the barrel. The gunner's assistant was blown back, and one of his hands severed. The battalion commander shouted through the color of smoke... "Run your platoon to the cottage!"

This was then a big clash. The wounded were lying in the ditches by the coconut palms. Toan was standing in a trench, pointing and shouting. To the left in the distance, there was the sound of grenades exploding and shouts calling for assault.

My platoon pushed to the right. The direction of the advance was now perpendicular to the canals, so we could only jump in long steps on the banks of the canals–one jump missing and I fell into the ditch with two light soldiers. Crawling up from the grassy slope, I saw two Viet Cong corpses lying on the ground. One body was smashed to the chest, the other body lying face down, unconscious... Dead men, the first time I touched - An enemy's corpse.

"Come on, guys!" I shouted. "Whoever hides behind me, I'll shoot at your leg!" The slow soldiers tried to find a way across the canal. They couldn't jump over because they were carrying too much weight. "Fuck. Can't you jump over? So brisk normally, and now slow as a turtle!" I cursed loudly.

The platoon had reached the edge of the village and stopped to look out over the open field. Sitting against a coconut tree, I was tired of shouting so much, recalling the swearing. I had become a stranger to myself. The enemy ran past from the left, the shadow of a black shirt hiding behind the green coconut trees on the other side of the field. "Shoot! Shoot!" My platoon opened fire, gloriously. Several silhouettes in black shirts fell. The vapor from gunpowder, the odor of the mud, the blood of the dead rose up in a trance.

At six o'clock in the afternoon, the sound of gunfire from the left side in the direction of the 71st company completely ceased while the medivac helicopters began to arrive. The blue smoke marking the landing zone rose up, thickening the space falling into the night, and the green of coconut trees darkened. The enemy's aimless gunfire shot onto the helicopters as they retreated. I sat on a coconut stump, exhausted, as a soldier crept up to my side. "Some chicken porridge, lieutenant?"

"Chicken soup?" I replied.

"Yes, I caught a chicken," He explained, "still hatching

eggs."

"Well, give me an egg. I can't take the porridge."

While the soldiers in the platoon were eating porridge, I walked back towards the corpses of the two Viet Cong. The man lying on his stomach was now turned up, perhaps in the last movement before he died. I put my hand on the cold, dead skin. At night, we spread out ponchos and laid down on the banks of the canal and did not take off our shoes. The enemy seemed intent on attacking again, so we had to be on guard.

The battalion continued the pursuit. Today my company took the lead, my platoon led the company, we walked along a large canal where the green coconut range spread as far as the eye could see. The village seemed well off, but no one was in sight. We were cautious every step of the way.

"The tunnel shows human footprints! Spread around, only one person come up to see," I ordered.

"Who's down below, come up!" Weighted silence.

"Up, or I'll throw a grenade down! Lieutenant, let me throw the grenade down," the soldier asked for my order.

"No, you just shoot down."

The soldier quickly shot down a gust of Thompson rifle. There was a low groan.

"Up or I'll continue shooting. Hands up!" I held my breath as a white head slowly emerged from the mouth of the tunnel, slowly giving way to an old man carrying an aged woman. As soon as he came out of the tunnel, the man folded his arms and kowtowed in four directions. The old woman fell down, marred by a wound on her head.

By noon, I was as exhausted as an arrow at the end of its flight. The image of two silver-haired figures crawling out from the mouth of the tunnel, the panicked faces of two enemies less than sixteen years old pulled from a bunch of duckweed, one of them still holding a bowl of rice... These images now added up. Scenes of the death of a husband and wife and their three children in front of my eyes. They had died the day before yesterday, when the enemy placed their headquarters in the church. The husband, being the sexton, had taken the whole family to hide under Christ's altar.

The Lord's statue had fallen on its side. The statue of the Angels had broken, leaving two white terracotta hands on the floor. When I bent down to pick them up, I discovered corpses. They had died sitting: the couple positioned side by side, holding their three children in front of their chest. They had died due to pressure, so their bodies were still intact, their faces painted with panic. I ordered the bodies to be dragged to the yard.

The church was now quiet. Christ's statue was lively in a leaning position. The sun outside did not shine in, and the air was heavy and cold. I sat down on a chair, silently asking, "God, are you real?"

When I walked out to the back of the church, past the living quarters of the dead people, a girl's purple shirt probably was still fluttering in the wind. Looking out into the distance, a girl's body was lying flat on the tiled floor, bathed in brilliantly shining sunlight. Someone had thrust a cruel knife in my heart, and I was gripped with sadness. I struggled to light a cigarette. The death was so tragic, but the image of the girl lying dead while the shirt was still blowing in the wind resounded in my mind like a miserable cry that didn't stop. The old couple from the tunnel, the young Viet Cong, the sexton and his wife–at least these had lived and died with a purpose and a choice, and anyway, had lived most of their lives. The girl had died unexpectedly, without warning, still loving life like the fresh color of the shirt. I felt dizzy and suffocated, struggling in an endless sorrowful anger.

In this big battle, the battalion got a lot of guns and ammunition, and successfully pursued the enemy to drive them to Highway 4. On the left was Tien Giang River. The 3rd Airborne Battalion parachuted on the right as a blocking element. My battalion drove the enemy from east to west. The Viet Cong dispersed in small groups to escape. Three combat companies were used to carry out a thorough search, without leaving a small crevice. The Viet Cong were dug up from ponds, rice banks, and straw dunes–the pursuit was both comical and exciting, like in a game. I walked stone-faced among the troops; the battle yesterday, a sleepless night, the mass death of the Viet Cong, the cadavers rolling around, all fell on my innocent soul in one instant, and I almost fainted. It was like drinking for the first time, but this was a black kind of drunkenness. I sent the troops into a large coconut orchard, one squad on the left, the other on the right, searching along the two small canals surrounding the garden. I went into the house that was smoldering, with big pillars scattered and sending up gray smoke. A woman in a white shirt and black pants holding a rattan basket in front of her chest sat motionless on the brick floor, her eyes staring straight in bewilderment. When she saw us enter, she rose up, standing upright like a statue, like a dead tree, with empty eyes. The boy who had followed me, as well as the tele-transmitter, snuck right into the kitchen to look for food. Approaching the woman, I asked, ""Why are you sitting here? Don't you know there was a fight?"

Silence masked her bewildered eyes, which flashed with fear. Suddenly, she brought the rattan basket straight to my face with the quick, neat movement of a gymnast. After a moment of surprise, I reached my hand out to take it: Two sets of female clothes, a headscarf, a small package of paper tied with a rubber band. Opening the package, I discovered two gold necklaces, a pair of earrings. "Are these yours?" I uttered. Still silence–stifling, strange.

"This motherfucker is crazy, lieutenant. Got to be so scared she'd gone crazy," the tele-transmitter whispered behind my back, his eyes shining as he looked at the glints of gold on the paper.

"Gold, probably more than an ounce. Take it, lieutenant. Hey, woman! Scat!" the soldier waved the woman away. Coldly, she turned and lifelessly walked away.

"Hey, you come back here. Take this back!" I called out. The woman turned, also in silent steps, back to stand in front of me, but her eyes were now bursting with fear–a pathetic panic made her face twitch and her lips quiver. She was still very young, about twenty-seven, twenty-eight years old, with naturally cool white skin, a little hair falling on her forehead to make her face more delicate. I handed back the rattan basket, and as she extended her arm out, it trembled like a stifled cry. The basket fell to the ground, revealing her two arms hanging down tiredly along her body. Tears streamed down her cheeks.

Pointing the gun at her face, I barked "Sit here!" I directed the barrel of the gun at the steps. "When we go, you will follow. Why are you crying? Pick up the gold." Silence. Only a strange silence unfolded as the woman's body kept shaking, her tears relentlessly flowing. Slowly she put her hand on the buttons in front of her chest. "No! It can't be like that." I wanted to hold her other hand to stop her trembling fingers from slowly opening the rows of buttons to expose a part of her rosy breasts in the sun. "It's not like that, sister." The woman misunderstood me. *Didn't take the gold and telling me to stop!!* She did not understand my words, those coming from a Vietnamese living in the same country as hers. She had thought I wanted her body and demanded rape! Poor me, how could a twenty-one-year-old officer know such a life of blood and pain and shame? I had joined the army with only one thought: Go all over my homeland and fight to bring an end to the war. How tragic for me with this shameful misunderstanding. How tragic for me, for the soldiers around me, because we soldiers can be brutal at moments–sneaky and greedy too. But we are not foreign legionnaires in our homeland—indifferent to the abominable devastation caused by this war. How can we have the heart to enjoy the sensations on the body of a Vietnamese woman in a terrible and painful breakdown? Poor thing. The woman of Kien Hoa province didn't know that we never wanted to brag and be violent in this shady green orchard. We never wanted to start an unjust fire to burn down this peaceful house. And those pieces of gold, your body here, who would have the courage to hold out their hands to loot and trespass? I wanted to put my hands up to fasten the buttons on your shirt. I wanted to wipe the tears from your face, but my limbs were stiff in shame. And you, too, poor country woman, what situation had pushed you to this daze of fear sending your fingers to unbutton your shirt, ready to sacrifice yourself to a young soldier the age of your youngest brother, while tears welled up on your kindly face so badly marred with terror?

As the soldiers withdrew from the village, the woman haplessly followed us, still numb with stiff, awkward steps, staring into the void without feeling. The Vietnamese woman walked in amazement with miserable happiness: Yes, happiness had finally come after the exhausted humiliation. The wonderful happiness like in a dream to see her body still untouched!

The troops retreated close to the highway. The river on

the left was full of boats, chaotic and crowded with people. Masses had steadily grown in the operation area that had fled from the previous day. The sound of people's screams resounded in a part of the river, frantically inquiring about the status of their homes, relatives, and people stuck in the operation area. A cry rang out: "Oh my God, all of Mr. Nam's family had died!"

"Lai! Is that you, Lai?!" an old woman at the river bank called out to the woman that had followed us. She stopped as if to recall a past, as though to remember a period of life that had been gone. "Lai! Hey, here's your mom!"

Lai stopped and turned towards the river, and began bellowing, "Mom! Mom!" I saw her trembling lips whisper, "The house was burnt down! The house was burnt down!" She walked to the riverbank, still with the footsteps of a lost soul, the color of her white shirt shining against the green of the coconut trees.

I bowed my head and walked straight ahead, scolding the soldiers who were standing there and looking wistfully at the woman: "Shit, get going and on to the ferry now." My heart was filled with a strange repentance.

The ferry brought our battalion back to My Tho. The people stood and watched in admiration. Stationed at the sports stadium, I went up the bridge leading towards Go Cong, the black water flickering with the glare of the lights flowing under the bridge was as turbid as my soul. Poor coquette provincial night. I wandered around, strange to myself, and met Bang of the Rangers, the smallest but loudest of the fifteen Thu Duc classmates joining the Rangers. Bang treated me to a rice meal, but I could only drink a bottle of beer. Then we went to the cinema, seeing the movie, *The Sun Also Rises*, admiring Hemingway in the book, but the movie was uninspiring and bland. I walked home late at night as the city seemed to be asleep early. A dry leaf flew in front of me like a girl's garment. Poor youth; poor me, too. Tomorrow we return to Saigon with the hope to take off our military uniform for a few days, but that was only a wish because we knew that Saigon was in turmoil–the Buddhists and the Catholics were driving their followers into the streets. For the first time in my life, I knew what it was like to be indignant when I returned to Saigon and stationed at the General Police Department, receiving a gas mask to be ready for quelling the protests.

***

The two teenagers in the front row held up a banner: "Hooray to the Army." The other two young men carried a yellow banner: "Resolutely Defend the Dharma." The crowd was estimated at more than a hundred people: mostly teenagers under the age of twenty, a few elderly women, a few yellow robes looming. My platoon lined up at the intersection of Tran Quoc Toan-Cao Thang, waiting for the crowd to approach. About a hundred yards from us, the protesters stopped. A young man broke away from the crowd, holding a Buddhist flag in his hand while walking towards us, beginning to speak. I could not hear him clearly, only faintly making out a couple of nouns: "Dictatorship. Dharma. Democracy," mixed up chaotically. Suddenly, he hoisted up the flag and the crowd cheered loudly. Shameless silence weighed down on me. The young man continued for a moment. A yellow robe separated from the crowd and stood next to him. The monk's hand was holding a small flag, and as he raised it, his arms were spread upward in a V shape, like a boxer going up to the stage to greet the audience. I couldn't hear what he said, because I was paying attention to the crowd. The youthful protesters mostly wore sandals, narrow-leg pants, untucked shirts. Two or three guys standing in the front row had long shaggy hair, their mouths chewing bread. There were a few girls with schoolgirl briefcases in their hands. But the most lively were the two women in black pants and cotton clothes, raging, holding a stick in each hand. One woman, while cursing, suddenly stopped, ran into the water fountain nearby to take a sip, then jumped back and continued howling.

A blue police car was parked behind us, followed by two GMC trucks full of field police. We backed away, making room for the police. The anti-protest specialists quickly organized into a formation, and the loudspeakers urged the crowd to disperse. A thick response of boos quickly responded, and a few people started throwing stones. The last call was unsuccessful, and the field police attacked. Bricks and stones, smoke and tear grenades abounded. When the field police moved forward, the protesters retreated to the Institute of Buddhist Propagation and became entrenched there. On the deserted road was a mess of clogs, briefcases, conical hats, sandals–all brazen and comical at the same time. The field police team got in the car and left, leaving the road for us. A new concertina wire fence was established right in front of the Institute of Buddhist Propagation. We lined up and stood in the sun and wind and bore a storm of wrathful cursing from the people behind the barbed wire. A guy with the pointed face of a mouse stuck his finger out right at me, trying to pierce my soul: "Fuck mother ass– how much money did you get from the Americans? When you die, there is no hell enough to punish you! Your parents gave you an education so you can kill Master with gun bullets!!"

Hot blood rushed to my brain. I reached into the pocket for the magazine I'd removed from the gun, wishing I had had a chance. He will die. But when my hand touched that cool metal, I let go, for in this moment, if anger were ignited, not only myself, but a platoon of twenty-four men would burst into a flaming, visceral torch. We had not had time to wash our muddy boots from yesterday's battle–our clothes and faces were still showing the traces of four days of grueling operation. The burn on machine gun ammunition transporter Ty's shirt, the blood on Thai's face and mine, the young man who had borne a lot of peaceful feelings in his heart, who yesterday had witnessed the unjustified deaths of a family. Only yesterday. No, I can't. I have to hold back. I have to quelch all the anger that was burning like a storm in my chest. "Well, you joined the army to endure suffering," I reluctantly reminded myself. A boundless suffering.

The protesters poured out again, now led by a monk in pale blue sunglasses. Arriving in front of us, he sat down to recite the Buddha's name, and the crowd followed suit. Most of them that could not sit cross-legged had to squat. I met the guy who had eaten the bread from earlier, who had one hand on his chest, the other hand reaching into his mouth to remove the piece of bread stuck between his teeth. After the chanting, the monk got up and approached me to ask to open the way for the protesters. I shook my head. He begged. Impossible. The old women from the North begged and cried and cursed to show support. Behind the gas mask, I thought to myself: "If I could kill someone once in my life, I would choose this time." The crowd cursed with the rudest obscenities interspersed with the chanting of Buddha. The name of Shakyamuni Buddha mingled with the filth of the world. Oh, woe to my religion. I remembered the death by self-immolation of a cousin in Ninh Hoa. *Who is choking my breath right now!*

The crowd started to panic and wanted to run on us. A stone flew from the crowd and hit Corporal Long in the chest, who cried out in pain. Suddenly, he hit the butt of his rifle right in the face of a young man jumping up and down in front of him. I immediately threw a smoke grenade. The rage that had been suppressed all day flared up like red fire. The butt of a carbine rifle swung around in front of me, and there was a painful howl. I shouted, "Hit again! Beat him to death! A reverse butt!" Human bones were hit by the brittle hardwood of the rifle with gratifying satisfaction. My platoon was in a frenzy of hatred and anger as we rushed into the crowd. I hurled another smoke grenade. Run! We ran back to the intersection of Cao Thang and Tran Quoc Toan. When we got back to the company, I took off the mask. My eyes were bloodshot red. Was I crying or had the grenade caused me to shed tears? Who knows, but my heart was a sea of sadness.

How would I know that on our graduation day, the life reserved to a soldier could be so brutal and shameful? I looked around at my fellow soldiers; now they were so close, *so* close. After the war, the soldiers felt strange to everyone on the outside world, and they were left, in turn, with only the voluntary prison of the collective to build up a world for the bankrupt soul. I've tied myself to this sad, violent world and become a soldier, tightly bound with other soldiers.

"Lieutenant, let me run home for a moment," a soldier in the platoon approached me and whispered.

"Right now, the protests are so chaotic. If there is something on the way, how can we find you?"

"No problem lieutenant. When I hear the 'coup music' on the radio, I'll know immediately."

"OK, when 'coup music' sounds, come back."

August-September, 1964.
Kien Hoa-Saigon.

Story 2

"On the Silent Battlefield"
or
"Communist Cadre, Who Are You?"

As I opened the door to the room, the cold air felt pleasant. The walls were brownish varnished wood, the floors were carpeted, the tables were lined with green felt–all reminiscent of the solemn tranquility of an American-style, a one-hundred-percent American comfortable place, with the clean, fragrant aroma of a whole mass of disinfected and filtered air. In this neat, clean little room, the thorniest issue of the truce–thirty thousand POWs on both sides and five hundred and sixty-one American POWs–will be settled, paid for, and weighed in hundreds, dozens, or individually, depending on the rhythm and climate of the four sides. Humans are left with only empty numbers. Prisoner, what are you thinking now?

Let me introduce to you - Captain Nam. I stood up and bowed. Eyes moderately open to assess. I am facing real Communist cadres: stiff, middle-aged men in olive-colored

Nam Dinh khaki military uniforms. These are core, mid-level officials who had just arrived from Paris, conference specialists who can sit for long periods of time and talk a lot on a variety of ambiguous, diametrically opposite, and pointless topics. The natural actors, skilled, who know how to control emotions in all cases. My first impression, judging from their facial countenance, was that they don't know how to smile.

The session began. Colonel Dat, the colonel of colonels, fifteen years seniority in the ranks, a man familiar with prisoners and prisons since twenty years back, an expert in prisons; no one could be better than he in this position. The meeting opened with the announcement of the day's activities, supplementing the lists of the return and exchange of prisoners on the two sides.

The order of speech rotated clockwise: the Republic of Vietnam, the United States, the Liberation Front, and North Vietnam. The debate was carried out through quiet, controlling, and restraining words. The reasoning did not follow the same system, did not answer the questions, but depended on the strategy of the two sides. The Republic of Vietnam announced the number of prisoners expected to be returned within the day, but because of the meeting time, it still could not be done because the Front men in Thach Han, Quang Tri refused to cross the river to receive prisoners and the prisoners in Bien Hoa refused to board the plane to Loc Ninh. Colonel Russell of the US raised the issue that the Front did not return the American prisoners in Loc Ninh as promised. The problems raised were crystal. I waited for an answer from the two communist factions, but the meeting gradually revealed the nature of running away–a comical, obvious avoidance. Colonel Le Truc, the leader of the Front group, talked about the list of civilian prisoners, and Lieutenant Colonel Tan, the leader of the North Vietnamese delegation, announced that the Hanoi government had just released another US pilot this morning in Gia Lam for humanitarian reasons: His mother was seriously ill.

Like marbles in free fall on a rough slope, the proposals, questions, and discussion issues raised by the Republic of Vietnam were distorted into other questions, general problems that could only be resolved at a future date. Answers to direct questions weren't obtainable during the session. I carefully listened, took notes, and my spirit became relaxed in a delightful coolness. Oh yes, that's what the new Communist "strategy" is about–never answer a question directly, whirl around in vain, as long as possible, and as far as possible. The clarity must be shrouded in a veil of obfuscation. Make it difficult, ambiguous for all issues raised by the opponent, even if they are only technical issues, procedures, distracting from the big focus.

Dignified like old civil servants, manipulating like skilled gamblers, the Communists dragged on the session in a deliberate and systematic disengagement. A four-year or forty-year Parisian conference is equally possible with these conference specialists, who blatantly avoid and overturn the issue in grave voices that defy undeniable reality. Colonel Dat brought up the incident this morning (February 12, 73) in Bien Hoa: the Communist prisoners refused to get on the bus to the airport, demanding to meet the North Vietnamese representative to pledge and secure their acceptance. The prisoners' representative stated that he did not believe in the reality of the Front Representative (Colonel Le Truc). The truth is clear: North Vietnamese POWs did not believe in the NLF representative.

Faced with the above fact, Tran Tan slowly opened the small notebook and cleared his throat. "Ladies and gentlemen, according to Articles 1 and 2 of the Protocol on Prisoners of War, there are only three types of prisoners: Prisoners of the United States and allies, of the Republic of Vietnam and of the Provisional Government of the Southern Republic. So in this spirit, and the agreement at the Paris Conference, we affirm that there are no North Vietnamese prisoners in the South." True to theory and strategy to the T! I felt like laughing looking at the solemn face, the sparkling eyes filled with contentment at Tan's sharp reaction in accordance with "spirit of the Protocol." The spirit of the Agreement, a fraudulent and intentional manipulation by the minds of superior swindlers, grounded and repeated with solemn words like a sacred dogma. The meeting, the unsmiling indecency, continued in wasteful time. Four hours went by without a hitch.

Ah, so that's the Communists, the genuine Communists–class A–the kind of cadre that yearns to become members of the Central Committee one day. Le Truc, Secretary to General Tra, Defense Minister of the provisional "Government" is just an "expert" who goes through three topics: supplementing the list of military prisoners, stating the number of 140 civilian prisoners of the Republic of Vietnam, and demanding the government of the Republic of Vietnam to add seven thousand because there are tens of thousands more! The three items were dragged back and forth by Truc, untiringly, for four hours despite Colonel Dat's firm questioning, "Why didn't you return our prisoners at 8:30 in Loc Ninh as promised?" Although the questions blared like sunlight in his face, Truc coolly paced back and forth between his three problems like a fish splashing contentedly in a separate swimming pool. From North Thach Han, a place belonging to the Northern army, how can Truc give and receive direct instructions? Poor Truc's sickly pride after repeating a topic that was far from the truth. How long had he been in Paris?

I sat across from the Communists, listening to blank replies, slippery arguments, snarky spates, and tasteless indulgences. I could see clearly the entire structure and tactics of the opponent's senior cadres–an opponent with too many myths and too many delusions. To see clearly and to reappraise yourself. You should not be self-deprecating, nor should you be self-aggrandizing. I conclude: These are just run-of-the-mill experts in language phonetics, in terms of personality and vision...just desk professionals that memorize lessons, and notebooks; listen to their superiors; follow instructions, working more with a trained memory than with the dynamic reactions of inventiveness. A team of average players specializing in teamwork with no right to individual creativity. The whole nature of Communist cadres can be summed up this way without fear of error. War and peace have been made and run by this class of senior cadres, replete with the obedience and determination of an arrow at the end of its flight; those who see the nation's tragic history through numbered and classified facts. I had faced a cruel and brutal opponent on the battlefield, and now I am facing an obstinate, relentless opponent across a wide, green felt-lined table. The barbaric cruelty on the battlefield and the extreme indifference in the room share one property–the generality of reactions, systematized after a long period of quantification and verification. I have not met Man on two battlefields; these are just adequate cadres who obey and hide their private sentiments in an absolute manner. The feeling hovers and gradually accumulates, like lingering cigarette smoke in the closed room. There is a flickering, haunting pain that never leaves that begins to show its face. The war has happened so logically. The Communists truly can only live in a violent and tumultuous world. Hasn't the materialist dialectic been a logic based on "explosion?" The room with a humming air-conditioner suddenly looked as threatening as the silence of a destructive bomb after it exploded.

February 1973

Story 3

"The Kaolo Pen"

I suddenly saw a whole chain of childhood days stretched out in front of me as though I was opening an old photo album. On my right hand, diagonally in front of me, Lieutenant Colonel Tuan Anh of the North Vietnamese delegation placed a brownish pen with opaque yellow horizontal stripes on the green felt-lined table. Oh yes, *a Kaolo pen*. It had been a long time back–twenty years had gone by since the day I graduated from elementary school, and it was the most expensive gift I had ever received up until that point. Oh yes, *the* Kaolo pen. The thing was heavy and large for my small hand, and I carefully twisted it around the end, with the spiral-shaped glass nib slowly protruding from the holder. The children around couldn't help but stop, and admire it. The pen cost thirty-five *piastres*, wouldn't mess up no matter how much you used it, and you can write in any direction. I happily twisted it back, the nib receding into the slot.

Twenty years, and society had undergone thousands of changes. The small boy who had never had a chance to taste shaved ice had grown up enough to witness the amazing twists and turns, the strangely impudent, instantaneous transformations that happened day by day, year by year.

Distortions in spirituality and in the surrounding world. Changes in the reasoning system and in perspectives. Changes in every thought pattern, each quivering chuckle to hide the stunned amazement. In 1950, Nixon protested Secretary of State Dean Acheson's policy of détente with China. In 1972 that anti-communist man slightly adjusted the hem of Zhou Enlai's shirt, acting far beyond the need of diplomatic politeness. In the same year, Senator McCarthy stood out from his peers because of his superior hawkishness. In 1968, McCarthy's spirit transformed into McGovern's stance. In the 1950s, the solid-wheel bicycle was considered a sign of wealth. In 1972 Saigon, Sachs or Solex motorbikes were called old and out of use; Ford Mustangs were just ordinary, though expensive, means of transportation. The Chief of State, Bao Dai, of the old days was now just an old man, even though the French newspaper *Figaro* launched an exploration campaign supported by a Saigon newspaper. Oh yes, Bao Dai was now a thing of the past. The Péron phenomenon was impossible in Vietnam, where twenty years of war turned all spiritual values and life upside down.

The Vietnamese, the most resilient race of humankind. And yet, the Communists in the North "seemed" to be unchanged: clothing, organizational systems, ways of conveying thoughts, reasoning, the way of smoking a cigarette, the way of breathing out the smoke, of putting your hands on the table, of fixing your eyeglasses. It appeared to be standard, familiar, as though they had been met, heard, and seen before. In 1950, at the war zone on the left bank of the Perfume River, presently in the Ashau region, I asked comrade "Uncle Nhan," "Why was the gun so big?"

The immediate answer: "Oh, the guns are used to shoot the French!" How similar was his quick response in this "resistance spirit" to the answer at Loc Ninh airport when I asked why the pants were so wide. "Oh, to make it easier to fight against the Americans and their puppets!"

Twenty years had passed and nothing had changed in those brains. It was the same old war of resistance: fighting against the sellers of the motherland, the struggle carried out by the workers and peasants, the all-for-unity-and-harmony brand of communism, a medley of concepts colliding with one another in a middle-parted hairstyle, with sideburns shaved clean. Lieutenant Colonel Tuan Anh possessed the quietest and most intellectual face of the North Vietnamese delegation, wearing a pleasant smile that seemed to be hiding a calculated and practiced intention. That cautiously quantified smile suddenly disappeared when he had to hear a word that went beyond the set system. "Lieutenant Colonel, do you think Indochina could become a Balkan region but with more progress and freedom?" Those smiles that suddenly disappeared often surprised the interlocutor, but when I saw the Kaolo pen carefully placed on the table, the nib coming out seriously and slowly, I suddenly understood. Oh yes, twenty years had passed without any change whatsoever in the North, with numerous strict and unfaltering systems. The 138 pages of Vo Nguyen Giap's book *People's War and People's Army* (Su That Publishing House 1959) was full of shallow and ambiguous arguments. On Page 112, Giap defined the People's Army as a "...real army of the people, of the working people, actually made up of workers and peasants, an army led by the working class." As Giap puts it, simpy, "The Party of that People's Army." And what was Giap's Party in 1930? Let's read the original name again: "The Communist Party of Indochina" Now let's continue to the last part of the argument: "The people are all members of the Communist Party". Fortunately, Giap had not reached the end of this reckless argument...

I was on my way to An Loc in June '72. I followed the Parachutists–along Highway 13, and Highway 1–to enter Quang Tri at the end of July, all the while founded by the same series of perplexities: How can the Communists be so cruel in such a clear-headed manner? Why could they have intentionally exterminated innocent people without any hesitation like this? But now I understand. Oh yes, the Communists had guided their actions in strict accordance with all the dogmas that had infiltrated their every breath, their every thought. Oh yes, the armed struggle to bring Socialism into reality was undertaken by the People's Army. It fought for the interests of the revolutionary working people, supported by the people of the Soviet Union, of the progressive and peace-loving people in the whole world. So, the people in the South, the people who were not revolutionary, not enlightened, and did not support that war must be classified as the enemy people, the "puppet" people, the kind of people that must...be destroyed! We Southerners, surely, would never accept such a strange, stupid, malicious corollary, nor did we think there could be such a devastating, rudimentary theory conceived as a guideline for so many acts of insane murder. But it had really happened, and had happened to the extreme–happened to the end of stupefaction. Mau Than in Hue, April-72 in Quang Tri, March-72 on the 13th Highway in the direction of An Loc-Chon Thanh. Even though I had been a soldier in the purest sense that had walked in the heart of darkness for a long time, I still could not understand the enemy's psyche that had reverberated in my heart forever, and ever.

But today in this closed up room, looking at the old pen on the green felt, my heart suddenly discovered the logic of the murderous system. What a shock! The Communists killed people through a definition. Oh yes, the definition put forward from the Autumn Revolution, further codified by nineteen years in "Socialism." Oh yes, the definition that was like a crumpled pennant flag put forward to guide the willful carnage. I understood Ngo Dinh Diem, that clumsy gentleman of the times, had to pay the price with a cruel death due to his inability to keep up with the changing pace of the political world, refusing to renovate his typical concept of direction as shown in his sticking to the heavy wooden table of the Louis XIV era. And so, how could a Communist cadre keep up with the modern world? How could he ever understand the minds of the people in the South while still holding an old pen in his hand? His mind chock full of the "sharp" arguments of Comrade General, a local history teacher of the 1930s, drafting the motto of the war with dubious arguments: "The success of the armed struggle of the people of Vietnam was first and foremost due to the Soviet Union Red Army's victory over the Nazis and Imperial Japan." Come on now, precisely because of that miserable victory, the French were able to return to Vietnam to sit with you at the grand banquet of Vietnamese blood for nine long years. And yet, that argument had been put down into words, popularized in smeared roneo-typed leaflets, disseminated to every village and hamlet cadre. Every "warrior" with his mind as closed as the raw bricks that were lined up waiting to be heated in the kiln, so that today, 1973, in Loc Ninh, in Thach Han, everywhere, we can only hear: *"Marxism, Leninism teaches us that war, the state, and society that are based on opposing classes will no longer exist when human society is no longer divided into opposing classes–when Communism has won all over the world!"* Marxism, Leninism, the October Revolution. All of them have now come to be only documents for research into a past historical period. But for "Lieutenant Colonel" Nam Tich, "Commander" of Loc Ninh airport, that ungrateful peasant that had betrayed his fields with glee, and with the "equivalent military rank," kept repeating that lesson over and over again. Is it possible that in that thickheaded skull socialism had been perfectly implemented on the military rank that Nam Tich never had a clear concept of in his whole life?

Saigon-Loc Ninh,
February-March 1973

Story 4

"The Women at Camp 5 Lam Son"

Then I...
cover my face and cry, my dear!
Bui Giang

The man holding the handles of the *"ameliorated cart"* looked younger than the two people pushing it because he had thick, long hair that curled at the nape of the neck, still blue-black in color, and his body still retained the solid appearance of a young man even though his face was ragged. His clothes were crumpled and worn out. He was in such contrast to the two men pushing the cart, since their appearance and pathetic ragged clothes were more obvious. The first, with a thin, high neck protruding from a Southern army's four-pocket shirt, now only the old model leftover, because the fabric of the pockets had been taken out to make up the shoulder pads, sticking out like two tumors. And the shirt was patched with various kinds of yellow and blue nylon cloth; where in the place of the two lower pockets were two sandbags (sandbags were used to build shelter against artillery bombardment by the South Vietnamese army before 1975), weighing down like a crumpled sedge basket. The second man was wearing a light blue jacket, the kind of *manteau* often used by wealthy, leisurely people when traveling to cold rainy resorts, like Dalat. But now, the elegant coat of the past had been cut short. The mutilated fabric had been transformed into a cloth hat that covered the head and ears–like that worn by high-ranking Buddhist monks. In the old times, this person had been a famous French professor, well known in Southern academic circles and formerly holding the post of representative of the Republic of Vietnam Government at UNESCO. It should also be added that the second man pushing the cart was a senior officer in the communications branch since the '60s, one of the first people to have graduated from the US military school of electronic communications–also of the South, or even of the whole country. But most people knew him through his accolade: the Southern table tennis player that had won the silver medal against world-famous players at the Dormuth championship competition in Europe, winning Vietnam third place in the world. Table tennis–only once in the history of the country's sports, Vietnam had stood at the top of the world until today, nearly half a century later. Now he was assigned the task of helping the professor complete the glorious work: Pushing the *"ameliorated"* cart. The cart was originally pulled by oxen, now *"ameliorated,"* i.e. made more compact and light for humans to pull instead of the animals.

The three of them were passing by the limestone kiln. There was a human form screaming in there. Without telling one another, the three men glanced at it, then looked down to the ground in silence. They felt guilty because of their helpless silence. In the past, no one knew who was the person imprisoned in the limestone kiln. The prisoners coming from the South when arriving at Camp 5 Lam Son, Thanh

Hoa had seen this prisoner in that limestone kiln–the type of rock that formed the foundation of the rocky mountainous area of Ninh Binh, Thanh Hoa; the locality had a prison system that had once been famously named Camp Dam Dun, which belonged to the Ly Ba So chain. Popular folklore still dictates its "hell on earth" conditions since the years of the First Indochina war (1946-1954). The security force of this camp once had the words "From rock we can burn to create lime. You puppets see how hard you can be!" The person who was in the lime kiln had been sent straight from the South to this camp shortly after April 30th, 1975. Later, the camp supervisors made an official announcement during a training session: "This is the director of Chi Hoa prison, an extremely evil puppet with bloody hands oppressing the people and revolutionary soldiers. But now on account of the Revolution's "policy of leniency and humanity," which is oriented toward education rather than punishment, he was not killed but put in a limestone kiln to have "good learning and re-education conditions." The identity of this "puppet" was exposed in a study session around the end of 1979, when the Southern prisoner in the limestone kiln had completely gone insane. The prisoners passing by saw him sitting naked in the lime kiln, staring out without feeling. "Eh... eh..." he cried out. Sometimes he would scream out meaningless sounds; his hands would scratch his body, peeling each and every blotch of the patchy skin. The hot lime steam penetrated deeply into the skin and flesh, turning him into a pile of red and gray flesh like a peeled shrimp. Today, the winter in the North was gray and cold, but inside the lime kiln, the naked man seemed to be boiling in the middle of the burning, scraping steam. The man holding the handles of the ameliorated cart surreptitiously sneaked up his hand in pity.

Then came the sound from another (ameliorated) cart,

pushed by three young girls, approaching them from behind with a menacing cry: "Come now... come now... you puppets stop and listen to me..." Even with a patched gray duffel shirt and a block of dry hair pulled back in a high ponytail at the top of the head, the three girls still retained the sharp beauty of their youth and their lively appearance. All three were barefoot, their ankles were full, their white skin was revealed by the tattered black pants. The professor felt a safe distance from the girls that he supposed were the age of his children or grandchildren.

"Hello, Miss Thai Hoa, are you bringing cassava to the farm kitchen?"

The girl pushing the right handle of the car, parallel in the same direction as the professor, who had just called Thai Hoa's name, expressed surprise and delight: "You know grandma's name, scoundrel?"

The teacher was a little surprised at the response, but still kept a natural attitude, pretending not to notice: "We know you over here, because on the last September 2nd party we watched you perform in the musical opera on the camp stage. You had a great performance!" The teacher expressed praise, just to win the girl's heart, for courtesy's sake.

"That's the musical *The Sun Bird's Wings*, my graduation project for an associate doctorate in choreography. The Bulgarian Board of Rectors at the University of Sofia praised me to the sky."

The professor was surprised and confused by the way she addressed him, but still tried to assuage, "You were so good, if you were in the South, you would be a professor at the National Conservatory. I taught there, so I appreciate the rare talent of people like you."

"Fuck the talent, fuck!" the girl pushing the cart on the left side howled. "She only has the 'pumping' talent, old man. Shit on your mother's grave, associate doctor in choreography and all, to earn some change for a bowl of pho. You will disappear right into the Soviet embassy looking for some experts to take off your pants, lie on your back, roll out. Your "fuck around" has nothing to do with "dance!" Your grandma here graduated with honors from the Moscow Conservatory of Music, and they still put me here because of a goddamn crime thought up by the wife of the head of the Central Literary Troupe. So now, not even a dick around! Fuck the damn miserable regime!" The girl stomped her feet on the ground while cursing, slamming her hands on the cassava pile to accentuate her words, just for fun. The girl holding the handles of the cart laughed out loud, proclaiming, "Now now, are you guys crazy if you need to ask them anything? Just say it to them. Why do you have to reveal your choreography background and having graduated from the conservatory?" She walked close to the man pulling the cart, saying in a jesting voice, "Hey, have any water pipe tobacco? Give me a pinch!" She extended the tip of her index finger to show the estimated size of the pipe tobacco pinch.

Gaining experience from the story between the professor and the associate doctorate holder, the person holding the cart handles replied neatly, "I don't have water pipe tobacco." And he changed his speed, almost like running, breaking away from the girls' cart. The girl holding the cart's handles refused to yield, imploring, "Hey! Hey puppet. The puppet– would you stop, if not, tell me…Stop! You stop and listen to my curse!" The person holding the cart's handles tried to run faster, but the two pushers begged, "Nhan! Nhan, slow down to see what they said."

"What did they say? They're slapping in our face like that. I can't take it anymore."

The man had been a well-known commander of a Rangers Battalion in the Mekong Delta, promoted to lieutenant colonel on the battlefront in 1972. The professor groaned, "Poor thing! Poor thing!" And as a reflex when in danger, he put his hand in the pocket of his coat and clutched the carved wooden cross that he had carried with him from the day he was in prison in the South–a way to protect himself and find comfort when facing difficult situations all these years.

The girl holding the second cart's handles was able to keep up with the three men's rice-carrying cart, and she shouted through her ragged breath, "Fuck your forefathers, you puppets! This grandma is only guilty of selling sex and you guys are selling the country! Grandma just asked you for some water pipe tobacco, the tip of a knife like this, but you were mean and didn't give grandma (she gingerly pointed her index finger at the face of the Rangers lieutenant colonel). You selling the fatherland to the Americans got you plenty of money, and you wouldn't give me a pinch of water pipe tobacco!? Fuck your forefathers, you men. The secretary of the trade union party committee was so mean…after fucking he only gave me five cents, just enough to pay for a bowl of vermicelli noodles. Shit on your mother's grave you puppets.

"I haven't got water pipe tobacco…that's all." The Rangers lieutenant colonel left the pebble road and quickly turned into the rice storage area.

"Fuck your forefathers! Country sellers! Grandma only sold sex." From the main street, the sound of resounding curses was mixed with laughter and enthusiastic praise: *"This damned regime hasn't got even a dick!"* Following was the high-pitched singing voice, with masterful technique, gradually echoing away: *"There's Hanoi, the faith, the love, the hope…of the mountains and rivers of today and tomorrow."*

The rice storage area of Camp 5 Lam Son was originally the Catholic Seminary of Lam Son Commune (where the national hero Le Loi raised an army against the Ming invaders in the 15th century), in Thieu Yen District, Thanh Hoa Province. Surely, the head of the Thanh Hoa parish in the last century had had the intention to maintain in this historical place the imprint of the faith–the transcendental and invisible source that had indirectly and repeatedly come to the fore with the patriotism of the Dai Viet people over the centuries–all were combined to represent the spiritual life of a nation that respects Humaneness and Faithfulness and protects spiritual values. After 1954, all the relics and religious facilities in the whole area were destroyed altogether. As a matter of fact, they had been disassembled since the outbreak of the war, on December 19, 1946, according to the *"policy of bare gardens and empty houses,"* even though the Thanh Hoa area was a *Safe Zone* during the nine-year period of the First Indochina War, from 1946 to 1954. The Communist rulers used the pretext of the war to regain independence to destroy the entire material and spiritual heritage of life, activities, village culture, traditional morality, and religion in general–but *especially* the Catholic community. The Sacred Cross, the statues of the Saints cast in reinforced concrete, the solid wooden church doors, prayer benches, and altar pedestals all "had the benefit" of being used as the foundation, pillars, covers, etc. for the fortifications during the war. When peace was restored in 1954, they became tools for the socialist construction in the North. Therefore, when they came here after 1978, the Southern prisoners discovered the sacred and noble objects in the cellars, composting stations and granaries.

The rice-carrying cart pulled and pushed by three people rolled slowly into a stone-paved path between two rows of arid and cold magnolia trees. In the old days, the rows of houses along the path were chapels or residences for seminarians; now, only the roofs remained (with the yin-yang tiles according to traditional construction), though largely dilapidated, and rows of columns were slanted and damaged because the stone blocks lining the base of the columns had been taken away. The professor, a pious person, constantly prayed, looking up at the roof of the dilapidated, broken, patched up structure and saw the shape of the cross in the cloudy sky. The Rangers lieutenant colonel pulled his cart into the yard of the rice storage area. There was a human figure sitting on the brickyard, its long hair covering its face and the back of a yellow and clay brown field jacket of the Southern Field Police force: Mrs. Duoc, Sister Duoc.

"Let us turn in the rice stalks." The Rangers lieutenant colonel named Nhan took the initiative to put down the handles of the vehicle, showing off his familiarity with business, and people. "What!" The person sitting with her face down, brushing up her dry, frizzy, tangled hair... The skin on her face was wrinkled, her gaze lifeless and dry...

"We from Camp D subdivision (Southerners prison camp) came to deliver rice," the person named Nhan explained. He adjusted, "Yes, we came to deliver the paddy from the agricultural team of Camp D. Can you tell us where to unload it?"

"Blah...grandma and sister," the woman sneered mockingly. The three men looked at one another to assess the situation, and, finally, the man named Nhan repeated once more, "We are part of the agricultural team in Sub-camp D coming to deliver rice. Tell us, sister, where to unload the rice." He emphasized the word "sister," showing seriousness.

"...Sister again...*Hypocrite!*" The woman raised her voice in a cheerful manner, without any hint of reproach. The three men hadn't yet fully understood the meaning of the woman's short words, partly because of the "accident" that had just happened with regard to the three girls on the way, even though they felt a little more "trust" in the "older woman" (probably of the same age as they) by her way of acting and voice pitch was rated as "not so bad." The woman pointed to a corner of the courtyard under the roof, "There. Put it down there. But hey, don't say "grandma" or "sister" anymore, you hear?"

"We've been at this camp for more than two years now. We've also been here delivering rice for a couple of seasons. We've known you a few times." The lieutenant colonel hesitated briefly at the word "sister" (due to the woman's warning), but pretended not to notice as he dumped the pile of paddy on the yard.

"Monkey wording. I told you not to call me "sister."

"So how long have you been here, miss?" The professor interjected with the wise, rationally-chosen "miss."

"Twenty years already!!"

All three men cried out uncontrollably, "Oh my God!"

"So, what year did you go to prison?" The lieutenant colonel crossed the line due to the impact of the terrible suffering of twenty years in prison that the woman had just uttered.

"Oh well. What's the use telling? That year, that year I was eighteen!! But have you got water pipe tobacco to give me a couple of pinch?"

Hearing the word "water pipe tobacco," the three hesitatingly looked at one another. Finally, the lieutenant colonel, the international ping pong player, asserted, "We're from the South, and we don't smoke water pipe; but if we come back tomorrow to deliver rice, we'll give you some cigarettes."

"Those with filters?" The woman suddenly became lively, as if she had already picked up a cigarette.

"Yes, we will give you some cigarettes made in the South. We promise you we'll keep our word."

"Cigarettes with filters! End of ideas! Thank you, uncles." The woman seemed to be immersed in the pleasure of blowing cigarette smoke. She became lively, fresh, loving: "My life is of no use brothers."

"But... but how come twenty years? Almost a lifetime. My daughter is about the same age as you," said the teacher, deeply saddened with sympathy.

The woman started her story, "It's like this," her voice sober and steady, "No big deal."

***

That year, Do Thi Duoc, eighteen years old, A girl of Muong ethnic minority in Cam Thuy District, Thanh Hoa Province, at the Ma River watershed, was assigned to the district's breeding team on account of her ability to wade into the deep pond in the winter morning to pick up duckweed and chop it to feed the cooperative's ducks. She had twice been proposed and voted as *"Excellent Labor Emulation Soldier in the whole district;"* therefore, being at the time a youth association member, she was encouraged to become an *"object of party association."* When standing to receive the notebook and pink scarf given by the representative of the women's association, Duoc had an emotion that caused her thick and ample face to turn red. She felt every strand of her hair drenched with sweat, although she did not understand the words of the president of the women's association: *"Strived to do good work. Mobilized all means. Took advantage of all conditions. Took advantage of all possibilities. Overcoming all difficulties. In order to reach a bountiful harvest on the battlefront of agriculture, animal husbandry, frontline support, a grain of rice bitten in half, to feed the South's flesh and blood, groaning under the shackles of the Americans and their puppets!"* It was also unclear what the pink scarf and notebook were for because she had no need for these two gifts. Also, being illiterate, she never wiped her face with a towel. But she was determined to become an "*object of party association*" by completing her morning work, diving into the deep pond to pick up duckweed, then chopping enough for a few hundred ducks–ducks being socialist property, thus owned by the people. Working people. These words helped her to vaguely understand: People are ourselves. But she had a question: "Why does the management of the cooperative sometimes put ducks in a basket and bring them to the office of the district People's Committee when they themselves weren't given the ducks to eat?" She only had such a vague idea because she did not have the courage to put forth the problem "more urgently."

"Until one morning," Duoc continued the story, "it was approaching winter like today. I didn't come up from the pond until noon, because I had to go to the fields to pull the plough in place of the co-operative's buffalo that had just died the previous night because of the cold. I was chopping the duckweed until I became sweaty, but the ducks were squawking like crazy in the yard because they were hungry. Then out of nowhere, "the guy' lurched in-"

"Who is the "guy?" the Rangers lieutenant colonel asked hastily, because he began to see the tragic beginning of the story.

"Well, that was my husband. He was a duckman. The high-ups arranged for him to 'form union' with me to implement the slogan, '*Three resourcefulnesses. Three Readinesses. Three*

Buildings. Three Oppositions.' Because he had some disease since he was a child, his legs were stunted and entangled together, and his penis was as small as that of a baby boy. He did not have to go to B (Going to the Southern battlefield), and instead stayed home and arranged to join the production team with me. The high-ups said that it was the appropriate 'standard of the combined objects' so as not to have children that would negatively affect the liberation of the South!"

Duoc continued in a lively voice, mixed with an indignation as if she was being unjustly treated, "As soon as he crawled in, he acted as if he were the son of God, shouting, 'Hey, lazy laborer! Why don't you urgently comply with the above order to feed the ducks on time, with the right quality? If you don't do your job well, I will accordingly report to the high-ups to force you to correct your mistakes, to achieve and exceed the target as suggested above! If you continue to do negative work like this, I will ask the sub-committee to take back your pink scarf and notebook. I am the planning commissioner keeping your labor time book.' This was the end of my endurance. I couldn't stand it anymore. So as I was holding a knife in my hand, I took a thrust. He fell down stone dead." Her voice was clear and strong. "He died like that."

"What are your plans?" The professor was shaken.

"Blah, prosy question. Then he just lay there dying! I still had a lot of work to do. The ducks were squealing."

"And then?" The table tennis player looked down at his hand and the woman's hand.

"Then I continued to chop the duckweed. Then, then... his old man got back from somewhere. Seeing his son lying like that, he started screaming, intending to run to the office. I ran after and gave him a thrust. The old man fell down, his blood spurting out in a spout. As I said, I had a knife ready in my hand but he kept screaming, thinking his voice scared me. I'm not afraid of anything."

"Then what?" The three men looked exhausted, even though the Rangers lieutenant colonel had been a seasoned warrior on the battlefield.

Duoc concluded in a low voice, "When I got back, I saw that the duckweed was still insufficient, and seeing the guy's bent leg lying by, I pinched it and minced it. After feeding the ducks, I took the knife to the office to report the work had finished, and was sent to prison ever since. Remember to give me some cigarettes brothers. Straight ones with filters. End of ideas!"

To remember the time of death/rebirth,
In Colorado, and at the time of Tsunami
To be convinced that Evil is real.
(December 26, 2004)

Story 5

"Surviving in the Land of Death"

April 25, 1983,
Camp 5 Lam Son, Thanh Hoa, North Vietnam.

He felt chills creep up his body in successive repeats. The chills of dread. The chills of death. The chills experienced because you know you are slowly dying while your body is still alive. He raised his hand to scratch on the wooden door of the cell. Actually, he had tried to shake the door, but because he was too exhausted, his fingertips only touched the rough wooden surface. *Does anyone hear me... Does anyone hear me?!* He wanted to scream, but only let out moans and groans in his throat through his teeth, which even though clenched, still automatically clashed due to the increasingly intense cold that invaded his body. His head was hot again as though he was suffering from a high fever. *Does anyone hear me... Does anyone hear me?!* He repeated his plea; his eyes glaring into the darkness that seemed thicker, and sharper. The moaning was gradually muffled in the dry, frozen throat.

Outside the two stone walls in front of the door of the

maximum security cell came the sound of the Southern Soldiers' fellow prisoners: *"Bye, we're leaving, 'phoenix coffee'... We're all leaving, "phoenix coffee"*. Phan Van Gioi's voice was heavy with the Quang Nam accent *(which he understood was intentionally for him to hear and recognize, by repeating the nickname "phoenix coffee" that his friends gave him before the date of maximum security confinement (September 7, 1981).* The rumbling sound of a large group of people climbing into the truck. The convoy started the engines, and the sound became fainter and fainter...Many in the crowd shouted at the same time, *"Bye, bye. We are leaving my friend!!"* He clutched his body against the door panel. His ankles shackled to the platform didn't cause him any pain. He didn't even know he had burst into tears after uttering that pitiful brief cry, "Oh my God!"

He didn't know what time it was, nor how long he had been kneeling–lying in the position of one leg extended, the other kneeling on the ground. There was a creaking sound of the door from the opposite cell, and a finger tapping on the corrugated iron covered wooden door making a sign: "Uncle, what you...You 'Z,'[1] do you hear something?" He listened, but could not answer. The person in the opposite cell banged on the door again... *"Hey, uncle, what you... you 'Z'... The people are already gone, can you hear me?"* He exerted himself to whisper: *"Are they really gone!"*

"But what else, a while ago when I went out to 'work,' I passed by them, they were getting on the trucks, and knowing that I was in here, someone messaged me to say hello to you."

"Do you know where they're going?"

"To the South, naturally, where else!?"

---

1. 'Z': The abbreviated word for "Viet Gian - Z", referring to the collective Southern prisoners who were sent to the North after 1975.

"Who knows, maybe they're moving to another camp somewhere around?" he exerted himself, trying to cling to a hope that had already been extinguished.

"Shucks, there's no such thing. Everyone received *a ration to go by train for two days*, each person got a pack of An Thai pipe tobacco, and ten Tam Dao cigarettes. Only people moving to the South have that standard."

"So I'm the only one left here?" he broke down miserably, seeing himself at the end of the road.

"Of course, what else is there? Don't ask '*rotten*' questions like that. But hey, what's so difficult with you?" The voice was sarcastic, nonchalant. Ignoring the words of the person on the other side of the door, he changed the story to another direction. "Have you seen anyone in maximum security confinement like myself?"

"Oh yeah, plenty, at Hoa Lo, and in a few camps in the North. Masses of people are like that, from one period to the next, three or four '*concentration*' all along!" He clung to a miserable consolation: "But that's only for criminals like you, isn't it?"

"What to say about us criminals!? After finishing '*school*' [2] we go to all kinds of camps–after Camp 1 Pho Lu, then Camp 3 Nghe Tinh, then Camp Ngoc, Camp Phong Quang, and now 'our troops' go back to Camp 5 Lam Son. After the time at the camps, released for a few months, we caused more incidents, then got back to confinement, and yet '*Still so beautiful our life, still so beautiful our love... No matter how heavy the shackles we carry!*'"[3] The guy changed his voice, becoming serious: "I mean, I'm talking about political

---

2. *School: "Study-Work School" - Jail for boys and girls (adolescents) managed by the "education" security police force - After "School", sent to Camp (Prison).*
3. *Parody of a propaganda song in the North before 1975.*

men. There was a man from Hoa Lo who was moved to Phong Quang Camp a few years back, when I was still there. The man by such and such name, was sent to concentration camp on *'the crime of writing poetry'* for decades. The man that even had the guts to throw a book of poems into a foreign embassy!"

Turning his shackles into a U-shaped position, he knelt down on the platform, his head down on his chest, uttering: *"O Holy Spirits, please protect and help me through these tribulations. Let me pray for '**the unknown brother.**' Let me pray for the unknown '**Poet**,' for all those downtrodden in utter desperation and suffering."* His heart gradually became flooded with warm consolation. "There are people that had suffered more than myself, my Northern compatriots who had had to bear the Communist calamity for a long time; those who had overcome life in the midst of fire and death, enduring the immeasurable humiliation of this terrible dehumanizing regime - Inspired by, and with the Poetry Writer - The way to fiercely fight for survival in the land of Death. With The Word."

Story 6

The Boy Died on the River of his Homeland[1]

The two boys had no time to admire the glorious scenery when the lights had just been turned on in Saigon. The electric lamps from the naval yard ran along the harbor, undulating, glittering on the reflections of the floors of the high rise buildings, becoming apparent as the golden brownish sun drifted slowly toward the sea and darkness began to chill the river. From Thu Thiem, the boys took refuge in the darkness, crossed the river, rowed towards Thi Nghe canal, where the river turned a wide curve, merging with the Dong Nai river before emptying into the sea. "Are we being too soon, Hai?" The little boy anxiously and breathlessly asked his brother as he tried to raise the oar to bring the dinghy above the crest of the waves that were getting stronger and stronger because they had rowed against the frenzied tide that was sweeping into the sea. "No, the guards often don't pay attention at this time, they are into their drinking bouts. If we go late, we can easily be seen by the soldiers 'cause there would be no one left in the river at that time. The grown-ups

---

1. *The story draws inspiration from the music and lyrics of 'The Boy Bailing Oil' by Phan Van Hung heard incidentally.*

would also be coming in droves, so how could we kids squeeze in..." The elder brother stopped talking, lifting himself off the deck of the boat to steady the steering wheel that was jerked up because of a large iron boat passing by. The murky darkness of the hull darkened the somber night on the black river. "Hey Hai..." the younger brother started again. He realized something was wrong in the midst of this painful silence. "Stop talking, I'm stuck at the wheel, don't you see... Always asking!" the brother raised his voice in exasperation. But when the boat had drifted down with the waves, he realized through the darkness that the thin little body of his brother was morosely shifting, and his heart swelled with emotion. Poor boy, their mother had died when he was still young, and when their youngest brother was still a toddler. And he recalled the scene on the way back from Ong Lanh Bridge Market, when he saw the two younger siblings sitting huddled beside the cadaver of a woman that had just passed away. The mother lay flipped over on a pile of coconut shells mixed in dirty muddy garbage, her dull immobile eyes staring up at the bottom of the bridge that was pulsating under the weight of the convoy of trucks and tricycles, and the shifting mass of people in commotion above. As he pulled the two stinky little bodies out of the dead woman's reach, he looked down at his mother's eyes that were staring dry... "You go now, Mom!" Not a single cry, not even his own, though he was old enough to understand the pain of losing a mother. Every afternoon when rowing across the river, looking toward Ben Nghe canal, remembering the past year, it felt like the incident had just, is now,... happening... He always felt heavy in his chest. He was fourteen then and this little brother seven. "If the catch is good, what do you want your Hai to buy you?" he asked his brother in an emotional manner, his heart melting with a loving empathy. Poor boy, he never had had a full meal! He loved his brother because he understood the hunger that was always causing cramps inside his body. "I want nothing at all. Just want Mommy... With her by our side, we have everything. Don't you remember the time she fed us noodle soup with clear broth!" the younger brother became alive, speaking excitedly as if he were eating that strange delicacy, and the mother sat and watched him beaming with joy. "Oh yeah, and with Daddy, we have even more." the older brother's voice became hoarse as though he had to swallow something bitter, hard, oversized. "How would I know, and what did Daddy do, where is he, how come he's not with Mommy and us?" the younger brother inquired. Indeed, he had not heard or been aware of his father's whereabouts for a long time. "You just need to know that much for now. When you grow up I will tell you, and then... maybe not." the brother ended the story. He became thoughtful, because he really didn't want to remember the scene that morning... The soldier stood in front of the burning barracks, holding a rifle in his hand, his back and shoulders weighed down with a bullet belt and two other rifles. The soldiers fired as they retreated behind the barracks housing their families. The women and children were scrambling, artillery shells were exploding, several structures were on fire... "You run away, take my wife and children to Gate C, myself and the second squad will hold on to this post, stopping them from coming into the headquarters!!" His father shouted chaotic words at the soldiers running around. The mother knelt down pleading... "Please dear, don't leave me and the kids..." The mother waved her arm and motioned him to come over and hug his father. The two younger siblings struggled, crying out of breath. His father growled... "You and the children run to the gate. I don't go anywhere, just run to the Church of the Three Bells and stay there temporarily." His father ran behind the trunks of acacia trees with the other soldiers. At the main gate of Hoang Hoa Tham Camp, the entrance to the Parachute

Division Headquarters, the tank turned the barrel of the gun, looking out devilishly for the target... Bullets were fired. Flying bodies... "Oh dear, my love..." his mother screamed... "Mommy!... Mommy!!" He also uttered a hoarse cry, unexpectedly. The baby his mother was holding in her arms squealed... This afternoon crossing the river in the middle of the night, he saw the fire again and the sight of his mommy spinning above the pieces of his daddy who had just been blown up. He had been living with fire - Fire every day. Fire every night - Even though he didn't know how come, from what, what for?! Tonight, he saw the fire burning bigger than ever. Just now, when he was scolding his brother, he was suffocating because it seemed that the fire was nearby, burning in his body... "It's almost time now, don't say anything." he passed the order to his brother. His voice was cold. He swallowed hastily as his mouth was bitter, dry. The small dinghy creeped into the midst of the tall, black hulls, lying quietly like giant satiated animals falling asleep. Now only the elder brother was paddling behind the wheel, the younger had the plastic barrel in his hand, he leapt forward out the edge of the seat, leaning half horizontally above the water between the hulls of the tankers lying in the dock. "Here... here, Hai..." the little boy quickly scooped up a plastic bottle of water, reached out his hand, and brought it to his nose to smell... "That's it Hai, I feel like this is pure oil." The brother hurriedly said... "You jump over and scoop, what are you waiting for now. When you're tired, jump over to the steering wheel so I can take over." The steady puffing sound of oil bailing was mixed with the heavy breathing of the stressed-out boy. Occasionally there was a whoosh of regret. "So much oil, so much oil, I should've borrowed Uncle Bay's dinghy, we could've scooped more, they must have flushed the oil in the morning." When the older brother started to replace the younger, the dinghy was barely movable because its body was stuck next to a wide barge. He only needed to hold the rubber tires used as emergency buoys attached to the dinghy's flanks. The younger brother being free started talking, uttering joyful words…"Hey Hai, you asked me just now if I wanted something to eat?" "Yes, say it." "No, I don't need anything. But if we can sell the oil, I'll buy our little brother a can of condensed milk, he has not had any since the day Mommy died. Will it be okay with you, Hai?" "Okay, let me see." The elder brother answered vaguely partly because he was busy, but also because there was something vaguely worrisome in his heart. As he crouched over the oily black water, he smelled smoke and flames blazing red somewhere. Trinh the Northern soldier had been pulling out a twisted cigarette from his pocket. Three number fives, three straight number fives! He walked over to the foot of the lamppost, to get a better look at the small blue letters printed on the cigarette rolling paper. He couldn't read, but that really wasn't necessary. Three numbers, three numbers, straight cigarettes with 'rolling' yellow paper… Trinh muttered as he looked at the row of '555' digits and the yellow metallic filter. How terrific, fuck mother US imperialists are so wasteful, metal paper is so expensive and they use it just to make cigarettes! He jubilantly compared it to Hanoi's foil-wrapped cigarettes, intended for high-ranking officials… Thang Long, Dien Bien… No way to compare with this 'three-numbered guy'! He lightly tugged at the wick of the white aluminum swipe lighter. Got to know how not to swipe it a second time, as the rising smell of gasoline would spoil the cigarette. He was careful, meticulously preparing before solemnly lighting the cigarette. Trinh the Northern soldier leaned on the railing of the ship, looking down at the river, hissing in his breath with pleasure as though his body was opened wide, filled with a mass of fragrant smoke. He stared into the distance, across the river, where rows of houses were speckled with red lights before turning around behind him... The city was blazing with light as if it had concentrated all the electrical power the imperialists and their puppets could muster. Hideous, why are they wasting so much electricity! He always had a feeling of awe and admiration mixed with anger whenever he looked at people's activities, at daily events happening in the South, in Saigon (he always thought 'Saigon' instead of saying 'Ho Chi Minh City').. Liberated, and they're still so wasteful, I wonder how they used to be when still 'artificially prosperous'? Just because they were so wasteful, we 'out there' had been so miserable. No one else could it be to blame! Trinh the Northern soldier had come to this conclusion with his comrades and himself. Suddenly Trinh the Northern soldier cried out in shock and indignation as he looked down at the river, between the hulls of the oil tankers, the form of two children on a stalled dinghy, pushed by the abundant current of shifting waves as some ships around them were leaving the dock. And real calamity struck... The cigarette left his lips and fell down... The red dot zigzagged before disappearing over the black waters. Trinh the Northern soldier roared.. Fuck... I'll kill you!! He jerked down the AK rifle from his shoulder with a fierce, powerful motion. Trinh the Northern soldier aimed the tip of the gun... at the human body. His pith helmet fell to the ground. Forget it! He clenched his teeth. Pulled the trigger. The bullets burst out in three beats... "Calamity, Hai... they've found us... Paddle away, paddle away!" The two boys instinctively panicked, the younger brother jumped back to the boat. Thin, weak arms were swinging, in rushing movements... "Hurry up, hurry up Hai, hurry up..." The bullets were searing red in pursuit. Trinh the Northern soldier pulled the trigger a second time. Trinh the Northern soldier pulled the trigger the third time. The bullets fell into the water, tore through the wooden side of the dinghy, and pinned somewhere in the flesh of the elder boy's skin. He bent half his body across the side of the boat, face down in the water. In the silent black puddle he saw fire. The fire flickered like the time with his father in that last morning. "Hai... brother... Don't you die leaving me like this... Pity me!" The younger boy wanted to cry out, but he was totally exhausted when the boat escaped into the middle of the river.

All around... The water of Saigon River flowing through Ba Son Factory silently drifted...

In remembrance,
One time in October in the South
(October 26, 1955-2005)

Original PHAN NHAT NAM - Translated KIM VU

Story 7

"Two Soldiers"
or
"After the Conflict"

Introduction

After April 30, 1975, in "for study" documents *propagated* throughout the South, the Hanoi Communists often used the phrases "American-Diem regime... Thieu-Ky" when it comes to the government of the Republic of Vietnam, showing such characteristics as…*"Carrying the guillotine everywhere... so brutal that the heavens can't spare, the earth can't forgive... It's impossible to describe all the crimes even if you use up all the Nam Son bamboos, all the ink in the Eastern Sea....etc."* And in that "systematic" humiliation, the ARVN soldier was of course "described" (by a very "quality" slavish literary system, even though the writers might have belonged to the generation of "protesting" writers with a new sense of innovation) through the image of a *"puppet soldier"* who specialized in "eating liver, drinking blood…" calling the American advisers "sir"... and raping dozens and hundreds of people in a single operation. Nineteen years later, the "American - Puppet Crimes Exhibition" Center on Tran Quy Cap Street (that is now Vo Van Tan Street) is still open to bear witness to an evil time that pervaded the South. And the soldiers of the Republic of Vietnam are still humiliated and cursed with injustice, resentment, and indignation–indeed, an enemy that must always be present in the slanderous media system of the Communists, even though that *"enemy"* is gone, has perished, is no more.

The following story proves the above words: A small, silent incident, happening in the dark, in the countryside between two soldiers. In Vietnam, of course. Because only in that sad country can these trivial, pitiable things happen.

One

He was always aware that he was *a suffering person*. The suffering was real, from a specific situation, full of danger–always prepared to go to jail, locked in a dark room and worse, about to be taken away to be shot. This terrifying situation was not caused by him. It happened at the same time with the fall of the South, when the soldiers were ordered to throw their guns to the ground, take out the trigger mechanism, take off their shirts, pants, shoes. He did these things in front of his soldiers, right in the eyes of the blanked out people. He undressed himself in the sun, in the midst of the crowd without hesitation, without embarrassment, without shame. *He had considered himself long dead.* But because he had not yet died physically, he had to live with the consciousness of waiting for that last painful thing. You live as Suffering itself. This is an "undeniable, irreversible" fact, the way the political cadres, literary workers, the "associates and assistants" writing books for their "big brothers," the press, writers and artists in the North and the people in the South proclaimed, if they wanted to be considered for "Progress - Revolutionary Progress." It turned out that he had lived with the Communists for eighteen years, so he was infected with their bad habits and wordings. Eighteen years to wait for something that is not so encouraging. Equal to the time from his birth to the time of his enlistment, thirty-three years ago. Eighteen years. Wow!!

He kept himself in meandering thoughts like that standing at the intersection of Cach Mang, November 1 - Truong Tan Buu (lately the Communist State had changed the names to Nguyen Van Troi and Tran Huy Lieu–names of the unknowns). He thought about the dead–thousands of people gathered to be buried alive in Hue in the early spring of Mau Than, 1968, killed by shelling on April 29, 1972 on nine kilometers south of Hai Lang, Quang Tri. The dead in Ba River, in the section between Phu Bon and Tuy Hoa, on the Da Nang pier, on the Nha Trang stone bridge. And hundreds of thousands, millions of people have taken to the sea, are currently being exiled in the forbidden camps in Hong Kong, Malaysia, the Philippines, or have disintegrated in the waves of the ocean. Why have they died? Why the indescribable pain? No one can answer. No one can find the cause of the disaster. The deaths are not caused by any perpetrators! There is no murderer in a country with a "moral" man named Ho Chi Minh, who was honored by UNESCO in a centennial celebration for having achieved the great cause of "protecting people." The language has come to the point of pejorative immorality and cruelty, packed with abusive meanings to the very end. *"Revolution."* The most cursed word.

As he watched the little boy put the rubber tube in the Honda tire, he had an idea. In addition to suffering from disasters, wars, and other harsh situations calmly, the Vietnamese people always know how to develop and transform the most difficult situations into usefulness. Becoming inured, they manage to do evil things so that these turn out to be a source of benefit. The plastic bags drenched in filthy sewage– that disgusting, sordid piece of trash that could make any Westerner nauseous–can already be an item for scuffle that could go to the point of killing each other between two hungry people. Just like the inside of this Honda motorcycle tire, which was pierced with nails, was a source of livelihood for one person, supporting the whole family. Who knows (...with a very high rate of reality), this little guy who is patching the motorbike's guts will become a professor, an associate professor with a doctorate, or a mechanical engineer. Man does not live on bread alone. He can endure slogans and the sound of drums. More than ten years of prison in the "Socialist North" has taught him this "certain progress." And a man can also die peacefully with a few words learned by heart, repeated over and over again–like the dog in Pavlov's experiment that easily drools when he hears resonant bells in place of the imaginary piece of meat. The Vietnamese communists were indeed successful, very successful, in mobilizing words and meanings. The clonal words under their hands suddenly came alive, smelling of blood and corpses. Mr. Ho's corpse in Ba Dinh's tomb is the cadaver of the *"greatest"* Vietnamese of the 20th Century - In the words of Duong Thu Huong - writer of many "noble" literary awards.

    The diners that were in high spirits, the boy that was patching a tire, the two women that snatched a plastic bag from the sewer in front of the restaurant, and the amputee lying on a wooden plank with four wheels. The man who raised his ten leprous fingers, smeared red and blue paste to the sky, his face down on the asphalt, shouting, cursing meaningless words. Crowds of people passing by on the street swarming with bicycles, tricycles, cyclos, Honda bikes and cars carrying state green number plates piled up around the man, causing a noisy traffic jam, and a seething dust. The police security man guarding the road who had just blown a whistle to a girl, due to some traffic violation, was jubilant when she (pretending to be stealthy) pushed into his hand some money called *"traffic violation fee."* Take the bike, pay the fee, start the engine. He joined the packed crowd.

Two

When he crossed the An Loc bridge, it was already dark. An Loc Bridge was a concrete bridge that replaced the iron one bypassing the East An Phu canal, following the road from Moi hamlet to Hoc Mon area, emptying into Dai Han highway, and went around Saigon in the north. Right here, all along the bridge, on every iron frame. That day. The smoke from bombs, bullet traces swirled deep into the ground, imprinted on the red paint, bent some railings, the iron arch on the left bank was half submerged in the water... The soldier crawled slowly under the weight of the backpacks, helmets, guns and ammunition. The man moved like a worm. The only difference: the worm crawled peacefully in the ground, among the leaves; the soldier crawled in danger on the hot iron block. Guns were fired from the holly bushes, on the opposite bank of the canal, where the bullets hit the bridge's iron. The soldier slightly stood up, raised his head, and looked around–his eyes flickered with joy when he saw his companions follow. The flare of joy flickered at the same time the light of fear broke out. Oh my God!! The soldier fell into the water. Sank. Red blood sifted through the blue water. The backpack was stuck to the foot of the bridge to keep his body from being swept away, and only the plastic cone bursting out of the iron hat floated along the water hyacinth sparkling in the early morning sun on the leaves.

That year, 1968, on this crumbling rocky patch of land, lay

scattered corpses that weren't whole. A dog biting a human bone ran and disappeared in the middle of a burnt-out coconut tree orchard. I didn't know if the bone was of the people, or the soldiers, the Communist soldiers, or the Republican soldiers, because it was just a bone from a leg, maybe an arm. The smell of dead corpses drowsily following the wind became stronger in the early morning sunshine of the year. The first day of the Southern Lunar New Year in the past was also a year of the Monkey, like this year. Today, it took five minutes on his Honda to go from An Loc Bridge, through the An Phu Dong iron bridge to the Dai Han intersection. That day, it took him five days to lead his soldiers away. Maybe longer. After all, the war was over, and the Vietnamese had bought peace at too high a price. In this price was the blood of each person.

On the five-minute Honda ride, he lived with the pain of twenty-four years ago. The only difference was that in the past, he had had teammates and friends around to share. It was the first occasion of the year when the sun was bright and the weather was warm. Tonight he passed this road alone and in the evening of the end of the year, in the eleventh month of the lunar calendar. The weather was cold, and the wind was blowing an unseasonably humid, relentless rain.

Three

Three silhouettes stood huddled together under the thatched roof of a closed hut next to the ramp up Ba Thon Bridge, the bridge that crossed the small canal at the beginning of Thanh Loc Commune, where his unit lost three officers when sending troops to advance toward the market. All three were of the same rank of captain–one from the previous class and one from the same officer class as himself. Every time he passed by here, he always remembered the image of Khiem's jagged beard, the victim's chin slightly moving when he inhaled his last breath. *In the same year of the Goat as this day. How long does it take to get rid of all the sadness and pain? Follow the stream of darkness here we go. The lost... The living continued the dream.* He could only think of the scattered verses when going through the life-and-death relation.

Three shadowy figures appeared. Who were they? This road is not usual for late passersby. Rural people go to bed early, which is also a way to save the lamp oil. He turned the bike around, pulled up to the porch. *Where are you and your kids going?* At the same time, he realized, the family consisted of four, not three. On the man's arms was a small package, the baby was only a month old, its legs sticking out like those of a puppy.

"Sir, we're going to An Xuong Intersection," the voice of a Northerner from the countryside, pitiable, lamentably made to endure.

"An Xuong Intersection is far away, more than ten kilometers from here…"

"Yes, we know." The man raised his cloudy eyes and looked in his direction to demonstrate the certainty of his words, accepting the situation.

What can be done for this family? The couple was still young, with a little girl in their hands and the baby lying in the diapers. "OK, I'll give you some money for the road expenses. Stay here, continue tomorrow. The road ahead is still very far."

He put his hand in his pocket to take out all the change that Giao-Thuy had given him in the afternoon to spend on the upcoming Tet holidays. He gave it very quickly and drove away. He didn't want to think, and neither did he know what to think, anyway. Those who had died on this road, down the canals, where the bridge was, and the living here–who had a harder time than who? The dead had indeed lost, but what did the living gain? He stopped the bike on Lai Thieu iron bridge, the one crossing the Saigon River, connecting Gia Dinh and Binh Duong. The river rose in layers of smoke, dimly around the bend in the direction of Binh Trieu. The familiar old beggar was still sitting on the bridge.

"Poor man, why are you still sitting here now? Climb on and I'll drive you back to the market. Who can you ask for money here now?"

The old man raised his face and smiled–the smile of a child that was carefree and kindly. "What suffering are you talking about? Amitabha Buddha, your life and mine have not been so hard. Get along...and leave me be!"

"Well, if you don't want it. I've run out of change today. I've given it all to the people down in Thanh Loc." He was tired and vaguely angry. Feelings of guilt and worthlessness.

"It's okay, give when you have it." The old man tapped the can on the floor of the bridge, looked down at the river, hummed a confused tune of verse and song.

"OK, I'm leaving."

The old man crossed his legs, sitting peacefully. "Yeah," he quietly let out. His eyes still didn't leave the water surface, looming in the distance through the rain, where the fire from a pottery kiln on the bank was flickering with red embers.

As he passed by Lai Thieu Market, it started raining heavily, so he stopped at a veranda. Crowds of unknown people, standing crammed, short utterings from voices muttering, lamenting. The loudspeaker on the roof of the information station was announcing the results of the harvest, production, and political news: *"Thanks to the Secretary of the Provincial*

Party Committee of Song Be Province and all levels of Party Committees who came down to work at the grassroots level and directed deeply and closely, the factory was able to produce good and high-quality products and complete the plan in 1992 ahead of schedule, meeting and exceeding the targets proposed by the leaders. The Thai princess went to Ho Chi Minh City, the delegation of the city Party Committee, the city's People's Committee, the Fatherland Front, the Women's Union, the Thai-Vietnamese Solidarity. The city's children presented the princess with fresh flowers." He thought of the rest of the road, the alley under the bamboo grove, the stove, the opaque yellow oil lamps and the silent house. It was so quiet that he could hear the butts of the incense sticks burning on the altar of his mother's image. He always listened to that silent sound, the sound of the night shifting and the deep river drifting far away. *"Amitabha Buddha, your life and mine have not been so hard."* Really, the life of an old beggar has not been so miserable? Drifting all alone, before long back to the market shelter, the familiar sleeping place, ending with some wine to forget life. And he himself also had nothing to call suffering; much the opposite–happiness, actually. Worry about what? Think about what? His mind was empty and spacious, without need, without attachment. Even a cottage such as his was also much more discreet and warmer than a dirty market stall where the old man slept, and surely much bigger than the porch where the family with two small children huddled on the distant road. The two children were so small. Oh my God! He took out his nylon jacket from his pocket. That last few thousand dong he had given wouldn't change anything. He turned back the bike, headed for the iron bridge. The porch at the foot of Ba Thon bridge was empty. He walked a few more minutes. Under the flare of the bike lights, figures of people were running, the children following their parents, leaning sideways.

Four

The baby collapsed right on the handlebars of the Honda. The man (in fact an adolescent, so tattered and silly because of his misery) wrapped his arms around him, with his bag pressed against his stomach.

"You let me keep it like this, OK? I'm blind." The voice was young, genuine, from the countryside of the North.

"Where are you from? Why did you Northern people come here?"

"Yes, I'm from out there. I mean, I was in the army!"

"Why has this come to this? Where did you come from?"

"I came down from Loc Ninh."

"What? From where–?"

"Yes, Loc-Ninh. The new economic zone is over there."

"Loc Ninh, An Loc, Can Le Bridge, Xa Cam...Chon Thanh, Ben Cat, Binh Duong...A long line of people carrying children running away from the enemy in 1972. Running "peacefully" in 1973. And finally running from *"liberation"* in March and April 1975. Montagnards, Kinh people, those who came to the South to work in rubber plantations before 1945, migrants in 1954. Why have the Vietnamese people run on this hundred-kilometer road on and on and on? Not counting all those who have carried their children, their aging parents, along the long miles of suffering in their homeland."

"Baby! Baby! Wake up, baby! Get up so he can drive easily." The father shook his child, but to no avail. "We had started the journey the day before yesterday, walking at night and resting during the day. I held the baby, my wife led the way, pulling along this girl; poor kid, just eight years old and had to go on a two-day journey, feeling asleep while walking. No money for a car ride, begging for food wherever we went,"

"Soldier, why did you have to come to this situation?" He dropped the question halfway, suddenly realizing that he was talking about something superfluous.

"I went blind on the day of the liberation of Da Nang, when I entered to capture the commander's post of the puppet army."

"Was there anyone there to fight you to the point of blinding your eyes?"

"No one did anything to me. The puppets had all run away. Just caused it by myself. That was because of the B40 shot at the engine cluster; it exploded and burned some bright smoke. My eyes absorbed the glare so I went blind right away–even the puppet doctors couldn't cure it."

"Which puppet doctor?"

"The liberation army caught him there. They had so many medicines, and the operating room was so cold. I had been so unlucky, so, in the end, I had to be blind!"

"Didn't you get any allowance because of your blindness?"

"Yes, I was hospitalized, then transferred to a nursing home. I met my wife there. Later, the high-ups took my family to move to Loc Ninh. Since 1982, it's been ten years."

"What to do in Loc Ninh?"

"Well, do economic business. The plan was for the new economic zone to grow rubber trees."

"What can you do if you are blind?"

"That's for my wife. I just stay at home to take care of the children. Poor us, I had to let the two older children go to the forest to collect firewood. They stepped on mines, the ones left by the puppets," his voice choked. "And these two children contracted malaria. I was afraid I'd lose my kids so

I left there. She's having a fever right now." The narrator's voice was calm again, seemingly a little overjoyed at finding the exact cause of the death of his two oldest children (that is, not a part of his responsibility), and having made the right decision to protect the other two. The happiness of a person who had escaped death, and was very content with the lost part of his body.

When getting off at the gas station at An Xuong Intersection, the soldier seemed hesitant. He saw the reason: "Don't worry, I've promised...I'll do whatever it takes. After the engine cools down, I'll drive around to get your wife–from there to here takes an hour, one round takes two. Don't be impatient."

"No, I didn't mean it, I just saw that you've worked so hard for us. I don't know how to repay you. I wanted to say–"

"Don't worry, I don't take money for the rides. Don't you remember I gave money to you and her at the beginning of the night?"

"Oh, so you're the one that gave us money when we were taking shelter from the rain?!"

"That's me. Not only that, I can give you more. Wait for me to bring your wife and child over first, then you'll see."

"But we dare not ask for more." The soldier until now still didn't believe what was happening, let alone something bigger. And just to be sure he lowered his voice, "Grandpa, let me be impertinent..."

"Just say it."

"Are you a cadre working in some agency?"

He laughed in the dark, imploring, "*I'm not a cadre.*" Actually, he wanted to say, "*I was the one who caught the B40 the day you entered Da Nang to 'liberate' us. You lost your eyes and two children, but I and many others lost their lives, their entire lives."* He got on the bike after a laugh, and loudly proclaimed, *"My father has been in the army like you, but he's dead now!"*

He had told the truth.

Five

The woman holding the child stood waiting for him in the dark. Unlike her blind husband, she clumsily twisted and turned with her baby in her arms while climbing onto the back of the bike.

"What's wrong with you? Pass your bag to me, and put the baby between me and you. Remember to hold her carefully. Falling would be hard."

"Yes. Grandpa, run slowly for me. I have a broken arm." The voice of one coming from Quang Nam was sad and troubled.

"How was your arm damaged?"

"I... I was... *'the intrepid warrior destroying Americans!'*"

"Aren't you exaggerating?"

"I'm telling the truth. I still have a certificate of commendation *'Hero of Labor'* and *'Order of the Resistance.'* I will show you later.

"What do I see that for?" And reminding her not to doze off, he drove slowly. Heard and pieced together the following story.

***

In 1965, the woman sitting behind him was a twelve-year-old girl. She joined the crowd of people living around the landfills and the U.S. bases in Quang Nam, Da Nang, where the first U.S. soldiers landed, on Nam O beach. From there, the US army expanded the defensive perimeter around Da Nang, occupied the high altitudes on the Tuong Phuoc mountain range, the traffic nodes leading to the city, on the north side of the airport. Every day, the little girl carried two bottles of Coke in her hands to come sell to the armored soldiers protecting the engineering team building Cam Le Bridge, across the Thu Bon river branch flowing through Da Nang around the foot of Non Nuoc mountain. The soda was only sold occasionally, but every day she came home with packs of candy and chocolate wrapped in colorful, glossy paper. The American soldiers loved children. She had a delicate face, and the dry hair covering half of her face did not make her lose her liveliness. The armored soldiers and engineer soldiers gradually got acquainted with the girl, putting her on the tank turret, letting her hide in the metal domes (ready to make culverts) when it rained. They called her "baby Coke." At first she didn't understand, then she got used to it. She also learned and called out funny names...Bob, John, or something like 'low,' 'mellow," etc. And the girl also gradually got used to the unknown work–pouring sand into the barrel of a gun, stuffing small plastic bags containing some kind of water into the holes of generators, plows, dynamometers, and transmission machines. All were told by her mother after a period of 'research.' 'Research' was Uncle Sau Co's word to her mother on numerous times. After a period of "research" and accurate implementation of the above instructions, the girl was loved and spoiled by her mother more than her siblings. When the bridge was finished, the engineer soldiers went away while the armored soldiers stayed, doing their daily tasks along the road and around the base. There were soldiers walking along both sides of the road following the convoy.

There were often loud explosions. The American soldiers shot aimlessly. Armored vehicles rushed into the fields and helicopters flew by the sand beach, over the rice fields. The girl knew from where and by whom the explosion came. She felt a mixture of joy and sadness."

"In 1968, the girl had become a smart girl who did not sell Coke anymore, but washed cars on the sand dune at the foot of the bridge. She earned money quite easily and the work was not too hard. Mother even allowed the child to be intimate with the young soldiers. The blonde-haired, blue-eyed soldiers often said in a joking tone, *'I love you, baby.'* She didn't understand the meaning of the words, but it must have been a delightful idea, so she just shook her head and smiled brightly. She also showed affection for the soldiers by washing their cars thoroughly, returning the overpriced coins, but also knew how to avoid misinterpreted eye contact by switching to stern stares, and quickly evading herself from the lewd fingers and hands."

"Due to her job, she gradually became acquainted with the time, number of cars, and specific people moving in and out through Cam Le Bridge. The explosions thus became more precise and efficient. On the surface of the sand, traces of sifted human blood lasted until a few days later."

"But it was all because of me," the woman concluded.

"How?" He changed his way of addressing her because of a vague apprehension, a sudden tiredness, so the question was cold, and empty.

"Because I was so greedy! Seeing that the uncles complimented me so heartily, that day instead of just burying one, I tied up another block of beta, the detonator was touched, my hand was cut off."

"After the detonator exploded, who took you to the

emergency room?"

"The Americans. They often went out to guard the road, wash the cars. They called in a helicopter, which landed right on the minefield. The mines detonated and the chopper was blown up. The American machine gunner died instantly on top of me, so I only got my arm injured. It was damaged because of this second explosion, broken up to the shoulder."

"Then what?"

"I was taken to the American hospital, then transferred to the puppet prison."

"Why the American hospital?"

"Because...because...they didn't know that I buried the mines and did the previous things. Every day, an American nurse who knew Vietnamese would come in to tell stories, give me a bunch of flowers, and many toys, but then the puppets knew. They came to the hospital to take me away."

"The Americans didn't say anything to you?"

"At first, they didn't let me go; but then the nurse said that because I was a 'vi-xi,' I had to be returned to the puppet side. The Saigon soldiers locked me up in Bien Hoa. In the prison, I was allowed to join the youth union, then later the Party chaired by the Tan Hiep prison cell. My aunts told me I was another *'Sister Ba Dinh'* or *'Aunt Nguyen Thi Rieng'* from the heroic land of Quang."

"How long were you in prison?" He was bored, thinking he was dragging the sloppy weight in vain.

"About three years later, in 1973, the puppets returned me to the provisional government of the Republic of South Vietnam in Quang Ngai. On the day of the liberation of Da Nang, I went to take over the city and was assigned to work at the war invalids convalescence camp. I met my husband there, and the high-ups announced the marriage union for us. The hospital management told us that we were *'advanced examples'* of the youth of the Ho Chi Minh era." (Slippery words and phrases that didn't stumble...)

"You two only got so much?!!" He felt a melancholy anger, for them and for himself.

"I was praised, got a *'resistant warrior medal,'* and was awarded the title of *'intrepid warrior destroying Americans.'*" Her voice became strong and excited: "In 1981, I was proposed by the Party Committee of Quang Nam and Da Nang to be a youth delegate to attend the world festival in Havana; if I hadn't had debris from the mines causing melasma on my face and I was more literate, I would have given a speech at the congress, not Ms. Vo Thi Thang. But I was able to take pictures with *'aunt Ba Dinh'* and comrade *'phi-đen-cat-sit-trô.'*" Her voice was filled with joy.

"You still have the picture there?" He asked blandly not out of curiosity, but because the story could not be ended.

"Yes, they had made many copies the size of half a window hanging at the Youth House, the Headquarters of the Provincial People's Committee, the Women's Union, the Youth Union and the Children's Culture House. They were collective property, not mine alone. The senior uncles say so and I had to obey."

"Since when did you go to Loc Ninh?" He wanted to end the story because he had reached the point where there was no more joy. How to quickly end the pain!

"After I returned from Cuba, the uncles above obeyed the leaders' resolutions, following Uncle Ho's teachings, *'Where there's need, young people are there. Whatever is hard, young people are there.'* Loc Ninh was a newly liberated area that was heavily affected by the war, so there was need for cadres as a basic frame, especially for propaganda among youth." Familiar words flowed out quickly, as the woman had forgotten her broken arm, her disabled husband, her two children killed by landmines, the baby and girl with malaria, the hundred kilometer-long distance from Loc Ninh and the future that would start at the intersection of An Xuong.

At nine o'clock that night, he came to An Xuong Intersection for the second time. As the husband and daughter waited on the porch, he raised his milky eyes to look through the thick night, waiting for his wife and baby.

"Mom! Mom! Mom's here, Dad!!"

The young man stood up. He waved his stick on the asphalt, uttering, "You... You...Where's your mom...mother... where..." And when he had held his wife and baby in his arms, he burst into tears: *"Now I am confessing. Please forgive me. I had thought you wouldn't come back. You took my wife away...and...and I had also... wanted it! She and her children had been suffering so much...I couldn't stand it!"*

He laughed pathetically, "What and where would I take your wife and children?! I'm in no better situation than yours—maybe even worse!" In fact, he also understood the young man's thoughts from the first trip. There was no love in the lives of these people, and if there were any, they were very rare.

He took all the money that the couple had given him in the afternoon out of his pocket to use on Christmas and the beginning of the calendar year. "Here, I only have this much. You will keep it for yourselves and the kids tomorrow. The small girl didn't have the strength to walk, but what do you do at this An Xuong Intersection?"

"We are planning to go to Tay Ninh." The wife, after joining her husband and children, regained the initiative, as quickly as though she had possessed it.

"What to do in Tay Ninh?"

"We'll go...begging." The young man intervened. His blind eyes gave him shameless confidence.

"If you want to beg, you don't have to go to Tay Ninh. Why don't you go back to Saigon?" He didn't wait for an answer, and took off in a hurry. The affliction in his heart was too great. Seems like his eyes were stinging.

When he returned to the Lai Thieu iron bridge, it was very late at night. The rain had stopped, the sky was high, the clouds were silvery, the summer moon was blue. He stopped the bike where the old beggar had sat in the afternoon, looking down at the deep black water. The waves swept the moon along the river. The light of night fishing flickered at the top of the river, on the Binh Duong side. Looking left and right, the two spans of the bridge were silent, wet with dew and the recent rain. What to think now...There was a small boat bobbing around at the foot of the bridge. He walked over and looked down. His footsteps touching the floor of the bridge sounded murky. The boat was dark, only floating with a sleeping figure, with feet hanging on the waves. It turned out that the old beggar's words in the afternoon were true: *"Amitabha Buddha. You and I have not suffered,"* including the person lying drunk on the river below.

The last days in the homeland.

Written to all those who have lived and died on both sides

so that nothing changes like the river...

November 1993.

Before getting out of the country.

Story 8

"The Rivers Ran Through the Rocky Hinterland"

Introduction

When the ticketer on the San José-Westminster route (North-South California) put the DVD on playing Quan Ho music, the two women passengers began the story with a personal air of mystery, expressed through each facial expression, their voice pitch changing with changing emotions.

"Do you know how good this Quan Ho song is?"

"How would I know? My best bet is to hum to the tune of 'Honey, stay, don't go home.' But what do you have more than myself to raise this or that riddle?

"I know, when you and I migrated to the South in 1954, we were little kids. How would we know what they had 'in the North?' We'd be lucky to be able to maintain our old accent, not like that of those '75. "I'em in Ha Loi... through and through..." What with following my dad working for the Railroad Service in Danang, going to the Sisters' school at the Church of the Rooster, teased by my friends, 'Northern gal eating wooden fish, so teeth protrude out,' but still able to appreciate Quan Ho due to an older sister."

"What sister? Does Nguyet know things that you and I don't know?"

"No, this is a cousin from the North that I met later in the US. She came here to work as a commercial representative of some company or other for the Vietnamese side. I called her big sister (although she was younger) because she was the eldest grand-daughter of the eldest wife. She was very beautiful, just like Romy Schneider in the movie Sissi l'Impératrice."[1]

"Are you exaggerating? Even if someone from the North, the likes of Brigitte Bardot wearing a hat, or Jane Fonda's type, wouldn't look like anyone else. And what was it with your eldest grandma?"[2]

"It's this: my grandfather was Chinese, an original Chinese, marrying nine wives, coexisting in an extended family living like in the story of the Dream of the Red Pavilion. My grandmother, his eighth concubine-wife, was taken from Cambodia to Saigon, then brought to the North, so my aunt got that name. Can't you see it? That little sister of mine was born exactly one year after the 1955 event on Hang Duong Street, Hanoi. She was born in the year of the Goat, exactly ten years younger than you and me. And yet, her suffering was as high as a mountain compared to yours and mine, even though ours after April 30 was enough to leave our bodies broken. Look–hubby sent to re-education camp, raising the kids alone, crossed the border and arrived in America with the mastering of English the level of 'l'Anglais Vivant,' speaking broken English 'till the tongue broke, the hands

---

1. Famous American and French movie actresses in the '50s-'70s
2 nt

tired. But anyway, we still had the consolation of having lived twenty-one years in the South, and finally arrived in America. Compared to many people, you and I were much 'luckier.' Just imagine what she had to go through. I'm afraid I wouldn't be able to take it."

"OK, you talk, I listen. But with regard to suffering, who can compare anyone with anyone else? Who would say they are more or less miserable than others?" The friend with a deep, sad voice, seemed to be sympathizing: "Your life has been too much to bear already, from the '60s, '70s, from a young wealthy lady driving a Mazda 1500, then a Mustang Capri, taking her children to school. Then through '75 pushing a buffalo cart doing farming in Suoi Nghe, Ba Ria, to crossing the border to Thailand by the Cambodian way with two kids less than ten years old, in between the Polpot soldiers. Your story is scary enough to be compared with the story of Papillon. Then, finally, a couple more years at the Sikiew Prohibition Camp, Thailand, like living in a prison without a sentence."

"The story I'm telling you is nothing special compared to millions of people in the South. Yet that little sister's life unfolded in a different way, typical of the suffering borne by the Northern people, even though she was beautiful, educated, talented, and of well-off descent. I am not over-exaggerating things. Just listen to my story, then you will find that my words are quite inadequate. And remember, she always had to bear it all alone. Alone."

"Why was she alone? Where was her husband and children?"

"That is yet another clue to her life's pain—the biggest clue."

One

Baby Giang Thanh was as brilliant and beautiful as a perfect pearl. Born in a bright red sac (a "veiled birth.") in the Year of the Goat, she had *"no need of any wiping to shine."* And she immediately received a great favor: Contracting smallpox at the age of three. Even though she was shoddily treated with folk medicine, the illness went away, leaving only small scars on the wings of her nose, as if like a charm. The high bridge of the nose that ran straight up to the forehead showed intelligence and determination.

It is said that the maternal grandfather often carried her on his lap, looked into his granddaughter's eyes and said, lovingly, *"You poor granddaughter. Why did you have to be born a girl? Had you been a boy, it would have been easier to cope with an unrighteous destiny due to the inauspicious signs in your horoscope of a non-official star, with non-existing Earth, and Mars standing by itself?"* As a horoscope expert, he was capable of seeing the fate of people by reading their astral signs. He named her Giang Thanh as my grandmother was called Minh Nguyet, after a poetic idea by Li Po. She became the first grandmother, the eldest in a family of nine women from all over the world, belonging to many different races and ethnicities, that he had married on his way doing business around Southeast Asia: starting from Yunnan, upstream of the Thanh Thuy River, stopping and setting up headquarters in Hanoi-Hai Phong after collaborating with the chief of the French secret service, Captain Favani, in building a chain of opium selling through the triple axis of Kunming-Hanoi-Saigon. It was also because this Corsican captain[3]

---

3. *Corsica: The southwestern island of France, in the Mediterranean region, famous for its inhabitants with strong psychological temperament due to the harsh and barren terrain and environment.*

shared the same interests, - women and drugs - The great pleasures (added to maximum returns) the lessons of which he had learned, applied, and developed from his supreme commander, Major General De Linarès.

As for our Uong Dai Dung, although coming from Kunming University, an ancient 15th-century academy the great hall of which was reached by a 99-step stairway, famous as an historical relic of the capital of Yunnan Province, he clearly saw the futility and uselessness of education–especially in Chinese characters–something unknown to a majority of people. He was determined to get rich. Having money means having everything. *Money is First, capable of Multi-variable contingencies.* He planted, processed, and produced the thing that brought the most money: *opium*. And depending on the political environment and the military situation, he was also focused on another business, the transport of goods no less dangerous than the drug: gunpowder, bullets, and bombs.

He sold guns and ammunition to the factions that needed them, regardless of who they were: bandits, communists, bourgeois parties, not excluding extortionists, hired killers. Whoever he sold the products to he informed the captain, if needed, and this guy would restock him. By the opium den, Captain Favani expressed his praise, righteously declaring, "He is the wisest man in Indochina."

Master Uong did not answer, but stood up and burned incense on the altar. The altar was set up by the eldest grandmother, decorated with brilliant golden painted statues of the gods. "You are exaggerating, Captain. I just follow my wife's advice."

He had told the truth because the eldest woman had once entered Saigon carrying a rattan whip. She came to the house (Tran Nhat Duat Street, Tan Dinh, where later my family had lived before 1975. *You yourself have actually come to visit a couple times* - (the narrator reminded her companion) *the man had bought it for my grandmother, the elder, who had said with poise:*

"Don't be afraid, we're all women. I have to keep you on watch. The crime committed is the fault of this horrible man." She pinned the man down, using a certain martial arts routine (my grandpa was also a master in this, but dared not fight). He lay still and listened to his wife's vindictiveness: "She is young, only sixteen years old. You must know that it is immoral. I will atone for your faults by marrying her properly to officially ask her to come into the house. But now you must be punished so that you know what it means to be husband and wife and that you have repeatedly caused shameful insults (to me and also to her). This is the eighth time, the very last time."

He lay still, quietly receiving a dozen whipping as punishments, then stood up to take her hand, lamenting, "I'm sorry. Forgive me."

He turned and talked to my grandmother. When he returned to the North, he took his wife in a red convertible racing car running from Hanoi to Hai Phong, proudly showing a cigar in his mouth pointing up at the sky. The eldest woman sitting in the backseat laughed and laughed as if there was nothing to be concerned with.

"You still haven't said anything about that little girl born in the Year of the Goat."

"I have to make it clear to you so you can see what my grandfather, first grandmother, aunt (that little sister's mother) are like to understand how all that affects the genes from mother, grandmother, and grandfather. It is a combination of these people on the highest level–the highest in sharpness of temperament, happiness, suffering, even her very strange appearance. She has not only three necklines, but five."

"*And how was her mother? Your auntie…*"

"She was one of the first people (and a woman at that) to go to France to study music through the sponsorship of that French spy (who became a close friend of my grandfather's family). In the house, he was called Mr. Pha and only talked Vietnamese. My uncle said: 'He made a comment during a meal: 'I have eaten all five hundred kinds of cheeses of the West ('the West' and not 'France'). I have also tasted all kinds of sauces of 'Viet.' I know how to distinguish between pure fish sauce and mixed fish sauce. That means I've eaten everything without missing a single thing!'"

He sponsored my aunt to go to France to study not without purpose, for he wanted my grandfather's fortune to fall into the hands of his family. He calculated in advance that my aunt would marry his illegitimate son (that he said was an adopted son to avoid responsibility to the Vietnamese woman who gave birth to him, using the excuse that having 'high virility without semen' and being heavily addicted to opium, he couldn't bear a child, especially a son). This man was a second lieutenant in the 3rd Airborne Battalion, the unit that in 1954 had been the first to jump into Dien Bien Phu."

"*How do you know so much about soldiers and such?*"

"Well, Mr. Nhan, in my family, after returning from prison in the 'eight-nine' year, followed my aunt to meet him at Nguyen Trai Street in Saigon. Soldier meeting soldier recognized each other immediately, especially because there weren't that many paratrooper units. It was on that occasion that my mom learned about the case of my aunt, the eldest grandmother, and the grandfather in the North after 'fifty four.' The reality was even scarier and more horrifying than any story people in the South could have heard or imagined."

"Just hearing your intro, I've already seen what kind of mess was awaiting, so I can't imagine what to expect from the real thing. Although you haven't said anything about the other sister."

"Just take it easy. The story must have a beginning and an end, the coach hasn't come to Road 152 yet (the intersection connecting Interstate Highway 101 and Highway No. 5). If I haven't told you everything yet, I will tell Mr. Nhan to continue telling you and even writing it down for you. He had intended to tell the whole story of true people and facts in a novel. Also, because his friend, Mr. Do, the owner of Thoi Luan newspaper, had written about the suffering and pain of the Southern woman, he had to write about the Northern woman to be fair, and also to show gratitude to his wife's land. Let me continue."

"Before going to the South, my grandfather gathered all the eight concubine-wives and divided the inheritance under the decision of the eldest. The pots planted with wormwood at the foot of the altar were brought to a private room, the gold dug up, and divided into eight different parts according to the eldest's assessment of each wife's ability to preserve and make profits. I don't know about the other women, but my grandmother's share was decided as follows: 'Miss Eighth, you're the youngest, but you've proven to be able to replace me. You keep the largest part of the family, and you bring five hundred taels of gold to the South first with your offspring. You'd be the first to relocate. If something goes wrong out here, there's still a way to get around.' My grandmother was shaken: 'But you, sisters out here, you gave all this to me; if I can't keep it, that'd be a very serious misgiving.' The eldest woman smiled lightly: 'I am not mistaken, the day I took you home, I already had that idea. Over the years, you have single-handedly looked over all the Apatite mines in Quang Ninh,

Hon Gai, without losing a single pound. You were even better than Uncle Sau, who had opened such a strong waterway that was then ruined by the Cantonese clan.'"

"With the money, my grandmother and my mother moved to the South to expand their business, as you can see. Because my father worked for the Railroad Services in Da Nang, my aunt knew how to hire a separate train line to transport rice from Saigon to the whole Central region every week. You and I got to know each other at that time in Tuy Hoa, in the year 'fifty-seven.'"

"I well know the story of your family. Tell me about your grandfather's family that stayed in the North with that little sister," the listener impatiently said. "And I wonder whether you, your grandpa and eldest grandma were such wise and sensible people. Plus your aunt. Just upon hearing the story, one can find out that they were not ordinary people. Then why didn't they think about running down South? Was it because they believed in communist propaganda to have stayed behind?"

"I don't know if there was any political reason, but according to my mother's account upon asking Giang Thanh's father the day they met at the house on Nguyen Trai Street, the situation was like this: My grandfather said to the eldest grandma and aunt, 'The Uong clan was originally of the Bach ethnic group. The father belonged to the Di group in Yunnan, ever since the old days of the Tang and Song Dynasties. They had not been in good relations with the Han people in the North, in Guangdong, and in Guangxi; at some point Chiang Kai-shek had to withdraw to Chongqing to fight the Communists, so he needed to use the Kunming road to receive American supplies and military aid from Burma. The fact that Uncle Sau's riverboat company was so oppressed by the Guangdong, Chaozhou, and Fujian clans that it had *to go bankrupt is a lesson to remember, even though he had gone to Hue to meet King Bao Dai to ask for patronage and compete with the Chinese in the name of the Vietnamese. I had gone to Nam Vang, Cho Lon. In these places we can't compete with them (the Chinese of Han ethnicity), so I decided to stay in Hanoi. Moreover, I have had contacts with the Communist leaders (Chinese and Vietnamese). Thanks to my help and protection, they had been able to survive and operate in Mong Tu, Kunming, since at that time they had no followers; the Russians were busy dealing with their own affairs in their country far to the West, and Mao's forces were still non-existent."*

"*But that's regarding your grandfather and the eldest grandmother. As for your aunt, with her half French husband, and a paratrooper officer at that, why did she still decide to stay with the Communists?*"

"*There are other reasons in this case that I don't quite know, but the final decision was up to my aunt. She said: 'Dad has decided, so I can't let you stay alone, although my husband was an officer, despite also contacts with people in the Viet Minh (working in secret intelligence for many sides). Even if there were some difficulty, I can manage it alright. Mother gave birth to me alone—one mother, one child—and I belong to the temples and palaces. Only the Saintly Spirits can bring me back to them, for mortals can't touch me.' My aunt was a combination of the fierceness of the eldest grandma— my grandfather's ruse plus the education she had received from the years of studying in France. Mixed vegetables taste good. She had three sources of civilization and culture in harmony in the Spiritual Faith. But no matter how well prepared she was, disaster still happened as a matter of course.'*"

The narrator's voice suddenly went low: "*Things were quiet for two years, up until 1957, when Hanoi began to show their true face with the knocking down on the bourgeoisie. Those in the authorities who knew my grandfather and grandmother had all intentionally gone into hiding when the campaign started. The three-story house on Hang Duong Street one early morning was surrounded by a crowd armed with sticks, booing loudly, led by the neighborhood security police. They asked my grandpa to present himself to listen to the prosecution. He closed the door and told his kin to go out and tell the crowd: 'If you want to talk to him, you must be on the level of Mr. Dong, Mr. Giap.' But there was no need anyway, he had found a solution."*

"He changed into new clothes, a double-layer brocade robe, with gold buttons fastened on the right side, and took down the opium lamp, along with the gold-gilded pipe (which he only used when there were distinguished guests). He prepared the mix calmly, stylishly. Finally, he took from under the pillow the small pistol given to him by Mr. Pha with the words: 'This is my start-up gun. To the many people that caused me difficulties, presenting obstacles to my work, I use this gun to deal with them. It has become a ghost. At night when I sleep on my pillow, I can hear the cry of the dead. I'm giving it to you because (albeit when alive) you deserve to be the leader of these ghosts. With it, no one can harm you, unless you decide for yourself.'"

Today, he carried out Mr. Pha's words. After finishing eight pinches, the number of the wives he loved, he said loudly, "I am going now. Do not bury after I die. Burn my remains to ashes and throw them into the river. Remember to throw the ashes into the Qingshui River at the border, which flows to Yunnan. They are not worthy to humiliate me." He put the barrel of the gun into his mouth as if he were smoking another pinch. The last one. The number 9, symbolizing the Eldest Grandma.

As for the eldest woman, she stood in the middle of the shrine, in front of the statue of Saint Tran with candles all lit up, holding a bunch of burning incense, holding a skewer in her hand. She drilled the skewer through her cheek. The sharp point of the skewer poked out past the second cheekbone. She shouted as if calling all the soldiers to wake up. Through the light of the fire, behind the smoke, her face showed a mysterious majesty. The people gradually withdrew. Behind the altar, my aunt was told to prepare fuel so that if the people entered, she would set fire to the house. The whole family would be burnt down in the fire.

The listener was shaken, admitting, *"No wonder you and your aunt are both 'not afraid of anyone,' as shown in your protruding forehead* (the friend points to the narrator's forehead). *Ever since I was a kid and we've been friends, I've always been afraid of you 'going crazy.' It's scary to keep your mouth shut when you're crazy. Turns out that that was the way of the whole family on your side."*

"*I wouldn't have known it if I hadn't met little sister Giang Thanh, whose forehead was also upright, protruding like this* (The narrator tapped her forehead). *Even Mr. Nhan that had been facing life and death on the battlefield his whole life as a soldier was afraid of me, let alone you. But my grandmother's side only produced extraordinary girls. As for boys, they're nothing, including my own brothers. Now shut up, let me continue...but where are we now?"*

"At the place where your eldest grandma went into a trance and chased the people trying to rob your grandfather's house."

`"*After taking care of his funeral, it was my aunt's turn to join the battle. She said to the eldest grandma: 'Dad has died. You have to live to keep the house rules, but now it's my* turn to shoulder the burden. Not only do I take care of you, I also have my husband and children–this burden is my own. I can't leave it to anyone else.' She changed into a burgundy velvet dress; her hair was tied up, a necklace of pearls was worn around her neck, and she carried the property papers of the house. She got on a cyclo (driven by one in the family) and rode between two rows of streets with curious people looking out. She went to the Hanoi people's mayor and said frankly, 'Our house is the shrine of Saint Tran. He is a saintly hero of the Vietnamese people. Uncle Ho also wrote poems to praise him. Because the new regime has many rules, we know we can't continue living there. We want to hand it over to a worthy person who knows the value of the house. So, please accept it because you have known our family for a long time.'"

"The old mayor was shaken, aware that he had suddenly acquired a fortune that was too great because the house was one of the largest private mansions in Hanoi (only inferior to the villas, the French offices, and Grade A houses on Truong Thi and Hue Streets, albeit with much larger surrounding space). 'Did you decide that yourself or was it a 'Grandma' decision?' The chairman emphasized the word "Grandma" with deference, and what would I have to do? He wondered."

"My mother let me have full control and our family only asked to keep the shrine to Duc Thanh Tran (she deliberately used the complete phrase). She also let my mother stay to take care of the rituals. As for our family, we ask for an apartment in La Khe, Ha Dong and some gold as capital for business."

"What guarantee do you have for this case?" The mayor hesitated, seeing the rapid, easy deal.

"I brought all the papers here. Please give me a handwritten note to buy back (purchased the day before the army entered

Hanoi, October 1954) at a price that you yourself decided. We have had a lot of houses and now it's only natural to lose this one. Don't be afraid; we 'have decided to stay with the revolution' and not stay by force. My grandmother has sent the other sisters to the South. Our family remained to prepare the ground for the reunification day as announced by the authorities! The aunt knew how to combine all elements (political, social, private...) in an honest, stylish, but determined and tightly reasoned, voice."

"And then what?" the listener interjected, finding it difficult to visualize the event.

"Before going to La Khe, my aunt told the eldest grandmother, 'They (the new rulers) speak tough, but are all greedy and cowardly because they did evil things and are scoundrels. I gave them a part of the house, but you stay to keep the temple (later I'll have the opportunity to reclaim it). I'll go to La Khe so I can easily visit you and monitor the situation.' She applied to join the export knitting cooperative and turned to the trade route up north, in the direction of Lao Cai–Yunnan–the route my grandfather used before to transport opium.

"Having carried out the trade plan, why did she apply to join the export knitting group?"

"In order to have a household registration by profession. How could she sit still and hold a knitting needle? In 'the sixties' Hanoi started the war in the South, and my sister was just a few years old when she replaced her mother with simple knitting. By the age of ten she had mastered knitting, knew how to assemble the necks, shoulders, and knit complex patterns. The year the North began to be bombed, 1964, she had become a professional knitter exceeding the target–and in a month, finished three shirts to be sent to Russia."

"Then what bad thing would become of her life?"

"That's because I just told you in brief, but if I tell it all in detail, you'd feel so sorry for her! When we were ten years old, you and I in the South only knew how to play cards and ask for a doll, but she had to go herd buffaloes for the cooperative at the evacuation location (to avoid American bombs) and knitted clothes for her mother. Despite these challenges, she was clever and knew how to take advantage of her pleasant appearance to seduce the children of the countryside, cooing, 'I sing for you and you cut the grass for my buffaloes.' She stood in the middle of the field, with a beautiful bright face, her long hair blowing in the wind. Even though her clothes were ragged and she went around barefoot, Giang Thanh perfectly embodied the elegant beauty of the cultural North. She acted in the scene of Thi Mau going to the temple to fall in love with Thi Kinh; she sang Ly Tinh Tang, Ly Thien Thai in the scene 'gentlemen and ladies' in Quan Ho singing.

"How can such a small child know these songs?"

"My eldest grandma's last name was Dang, residing in Bac Ninh, or the Kinh Bac area along Duong River. During the reign of King Le, Lord Trinh produced the Tea Lady named Dang Thi Hue. The eldest grandma taught her mother, and her mother sang lullabies to her since she was still in her crib. Only when you heard her sing did you know how elegant and lyrical Quan Ho was–not to mention the touching scene when "gentlemen and ladies" meet each year after the Lunar New Year on Lim Festival after one whole year apart from one another.

"If life's like that, you can't say it's harsh and difficult. She could even sing."

The narrator laughed bitterly, admonishing, *"You sing to survive, to have food to eat. Not only for her, alone, but also to support her father, younger brothers, including my grandmother. In 1968, the Americans increased the bombing of the North to force Hanoi to sit down at the conference table. Troops moved to the South, the China-Vietnam border area was handed over to the Chinese soldiers to guard, and the Chinese bandits took the opportunity to sneak into Vietnam to make a living. During a trade trip, my aunt was stopped by bandits in the forest of Pho Lu, Lao Cai. She refused to give them her possessions, used a harpoon (with the esoteric martial arts of the Chinese mixed with the Vietnamese, taught by her grandfather and grandmother) to fight the bandits without hesitation. They eventually loosened up, except for one guy who pointed an AK47 submachine gun at her chest demanding gold and money, which they knew she had wrapped around her body. She glared at the gunman, scornfully, warning, 'If you want to shoot me, look me in the eye. If you're afraid, however, beat it.' She spoke in Chinese. The bandit closed his eyes, pulled the trigger, and the bullet broke her chest. The dead woman sat on the hillside, her hands clinging to the ground, refusing to fall, her eyes wide open, her long blue-black hair spread out. The gunman came forward, then suddenly clasped his hands and bowed down. When he recognized the Wang family heirloom brooch in her hair, he broke down, pleading: 'Please forgive me. I really did not intend it that way!' My aunt shed a stream of angry blood. She had died in an untimely manner, so she possessed strange power, and the people in the area had to set up shrines to venerate her."*

The friend whispered, "How did you know these things so well? She was filled with curiosity.

"How can I ever make up a story like this? Mr. Nhan was sent to prison in the North in '76 and came to this area of Pho Lu, when he accidentally heard the story of 'Madam Uong the Medium's daughter' fighting the robbers. She often made apparitions to protect people in need. That shrine still exists today, which is also consistent with what Thanh's father told my mom later. No one would dare to make it up if it didn't really exist. Thus, my fourteen-year-old half-sister had to take over her mother's burden of feeding the family, including her grandmother, elderly father, and two younger sisters. When she heard that her daughter was murdered, my grandmother just screamed in resentment, "Guns! Shoot... shoot guns!' She continued to live, but like a dried up tree, she did not speak all day, stood still in front of the shrine at night, completely losing her memory. She never cried.

The two women were silent at the same time as if the burden of Giang Thanh's pain was bearing heavily on them. *"It's horrible! Truly horrible!"* the listener muttered in a low voice. *"Then how did she manage?"*

"How could she live!? What a useless, superfluous question." The narrator continued with effort: *"Being cornered in misery, she became wiser and more prudent. From Ha Dong she returned to the house on Hang Duong Street under the pretext of visiting her grandma. Late at night, she entered the city mayor's office, and asked for debt collection: 'Give me the gold that you still owe my mother.' The chairman was not someone to be easily intimidated. 'What gold? I have repaid all to your mother. I'm still keeping the papers here. I only have my dick for you!' He looked at her with lewd, mocking eyes. Due to the mixture of three bloodlines, she was taller than an average fourteen-year-old, and her breasts swelled up voluptuously."*

"I know those papers, but those gold bars were much less than this house's worth, you must know! I'm not asking too much, I'm just asking you to pay some more."

"I don't have the gold! What will you do now? Don't act like a bitch. You came here on your own. I'll come on you right now for you to know!"

"You can't rape me. My friend over there is just waiting for me to scream so he'll run to the neighborhood police station!"

The mayor went to the window, slightly opened the slats of the blinds, and peered down at the street. "Oh my God! What do you want now?"

"I'm just asking you for the missing gold."

"What else?" The chairman got tired and gave up.

"Write me a note to the knitting co-op to help me continue my mother's work."

"Tell me all you want at once."

"Sponsor me to enter the Theater School because my father's background was not good!"

The mayor whimpered: "How old are you to be so dreadful!? What will become of you when you grow up?"

When lifting the lapel of her shirt, tying the gold rings to the belt of her pants, Giang Thanh looked at the man in a "sympathetic," complicit manner. She calmly explained, "I won't tell anyone about this. Your wife didn't go to Ha Nam– she went to La Khe to meet my father and won't return 'till tomorrow afternoon. I stated in my application for admission to the dance school that you share the same surname as my grandmother. You belong to Truong Chinh's Dang Xuan family, don't you?"

When sitting with her friend within the confines of Hàng Đẫy stadium, Giang Thanh cried like never before: "Oh Mom! Oh Grandpa!" She screamed like a madman. The boy frantically hugged her back to show comfort. She stopped *crying, gave the boy a violent slap, and kicked her friend to the ground.*

"Why did she want to go to that theater school?"

"Because it is one of the few institutions that give students many benefits and privileges in the North, with all of them concentrated in the Mai Dich area where there are political headquarters, the central performing arts group. In that organization, she would be given standard treatment with sugar, milk, and meat to maintain good health and a beautiful appearance. It only accepts around thirty students, per class, from among thousands of applicants, not to mention you'll have to present a good political background. Being the daughter of a French paratrooper, how could she have been accepted without the ruse she had devised regarding the mayor? Her purpose was to aim at the monthly supplement of sugar, milk, and meat along with the standard of sixteen kilograms of rice per student–the North's highest standard. Later, my Nhan went to prison out there with only nine kilograms of corn, cassava, 'equivalent to rice paddy!'"

"What the hell is that 'equivalent to rice paddy?'"

"That is the amount of nine kilograms of corn and potatoes; the cassava replaces nine kilograms of rice paddy."

"Paddy means unmilled rice! If you eat like that, how can you live? Only then will we know how precious and rare a grain of rice is to the people in the North. The poet Phung Cung had to exclaim: 'I bow my head. My hair is white, I break my head. O my grain of rice dropped on the ground.' With that standard of rice, my little half-sister had been able to feed a family of four."

"What did you say? I don't understand?"

"Well, that little Giang Thanh used half of the standard–rice–to feed her grandmother, father and two younger siblings.

For seven consecutive years from 1968 to 1974, she ate only once a day at noon, saving eight kilograms of rice, half the standard, to feed her family. Throughout her adolescence, she didn't have any sugar, any milk at all!"

"*Oh my God, you and I in those days only attended to shopping on Le Loi, Tự Do Streets to select new, imported goods, eating ice cream at Givral, Pole Nord–never at Hai Phong, Tran Hung Dao. At the same youthful age, why were the people out there suffering so much?!"*

The narrator whispered, lamentably, "*Not only the youth but the whole of North Vietnam, and yet how many people in the South knew about it? Only after 1975, when they had to suffer the same blow from the Communists, did they discover the truth. The people out there had been living miserably for many years. And not only concerning rice. During those seven years, she had been sleeping only after 12 o'clock and woke up at 5 am."*

"*Why did she have to stay up late and get up so early?"*

"*Well, she had to stay up late to knit, and wake up early to use the collective toilet and shower in the morning. Her clean habits as time went on seemed to verge on being sickly. When going to America the other year, she carried with her only bathing suits, underwear, and personal hygiene, including a foot brush. When she entered the house, seeing that the toilet was so clean, she whispered, 'I like your bathroom the most.' She praised to the sky the cleanliness of America!"*

"*So her life must also have been somewhat pleasant at times. How would she bear it, living from childhood to adulthood, that way!?"* The friend felt fed up, deliberately waiting to hear something good.

"*What I've just told you can't fully describe her life situation and way of subsisting. Life was so hard, but on the occasion of the Mid-Autumn Festival, she still tried to save up to cook a pot of porridge for the whole family."*

"Why must there be a pot of porridge?"

"In the past, when my aunt was still alive, and my grandmother was still young, and the holidays and New Year were the occasion for the whole family to show off their cooking and meal preparation skills. For example, that pot of porridge must be cooked with snakehead murrel fish, pork belly, onion bundled together, some dill, and celery. Before the Lunar New Year, everyone had to bathe with dried coriander water, wear new clothes to wish each other good fortune on New Year's Day. Then my grandmother lost her mind, my aunt died, my half-sister's father was in crisis, her two younger sisters were still too small living in a deprived and limited society of the North, so she had to play the role of the head of the family, the father and the mother all by herself since she was a teenager. 'My life was so miserable, sister!' She lamented to me when we met in 2005. She was then fifty years old."

"At fifty, she must have been awfully old, living the kind of life you have just described. Why is she considered younger? She's actually of a higher rank, is that not so?"

"She keeps being a hundred percent ceremonial, the way of the Northern people, not 'mixed up' like you and me (considered totally "Southernized"). Even my mom, not an easy person, had accepted her immediately on the very first encounter. She called her 'mother' sincerely and affectionately. Nowadays we asked for her opinion on all matters related to our house's business. Being innately wise, she grew sharper having lived a difficult life. But that's not necessarily the case, since the circumstances I just mentioned were common to the whole North before 1975. Even though for seven years, since

1968, it was as if every day she had to run back and forth on the triangular axis: Mai Dich area, Hang Duong street, La Khe (Ha Dong) to look after her grandmother, her father and the two sisters, and go to school at the same time if there weren't pitiful accidents, to say the least!"

"Oh dear, living like that is already too much. What more accidents to add to that!?" the friend hearing the story wailed.

"Well, for example, she lost her bicycle, even though it was merely just the frame and the two wheels. The robbers lurked in front of her grandmother's house, and like a tigress, she alone beat the two thieves. Then the third guy snatched the cycle and ran away. She ran after him, and was hit across the face with a stick. She had to use her two sleeves to stop him. Both hands are now scarred and injured from this beating, but fortunately, she could still maintain a beautiful face, being a ballet dancer. How would she do it with a scarred face!? With her bicycle lost, she had to jump on the tram many times when traveling from Mai Dich to Ha Dong, avoiding the ticket conductor to save a few coins (estimated at only about one or two US cents). But all that material deprivation seemed not to affect her since, perhaps, she had no other choice and knew no other way. If it weren't the accident in love, and love's consequences!"

"Having gone through such a miserable situation, what could it mean to be in love with a boy!?" The interlocutor voiced her criticism, really wondering about the psychological state of a person who had experienced extreme hardship, and yet not quite tough and mature.

"You speak like a saint. To be true, when your husband, Viet, came home late after his teaching, you rushed down to La Pagode to find him (a coffee shop on Tu Do Street, Saigon (1954-1975); a familiar meeting place for writers, newspaper

men, cultural figures in literature, the youth and students in the South). And assuming you asked with sincerity, you really don't understand her either–she was just a child who had to endure the harsh life of adults, which she had to take the place of. So, when she heard her classmate, the guy that had accompanied her to the city mayor's office the year before, and that was also the theater school director's son, express his love for her, she being a loyal, straightforward type, believed him and accepted his proposal immediately. Maybe they really loved each other considering their actual conditions, their delicate looks and their same level of talents. Plus the boy had promised his wedding present, a Phoenix-brand bicycle made in China that was being lent to her. She also thought that with her beautiful body and genuine personality, she would be respected and loved by everyone.. She treated the guy's family the way an official daughter-in-law would do–that is, she treated the whole family as well as her own, and partly because she was well fed and received a per diem every time she went performing in her last years at the dance school."

"One day, she brought breakfast to her husband–sticky rice cooked from dawn to show her love and care–by carefully balancing the plate with one hand while the other held onto the bicycle handlebar, staggering along in the middle of the northern winter. As she walked in, she found him sleeping with one of her classmates! She fainted on the doorstep, and a seizure; her teeth clenched, her body as stiff as a block of wood. The guy, panicked that he would be responsible if she died, peed on her face, as urged and instructed by the people around him. Awakened, she went away without looking back. Her face was cold, her eyes dry. Her cleanliness and feeling of disgust with regard to sexual encounters started at that time, and got worse with time. She saw the guy's genitals in *front of her in her seizure!"*

In short, she was still just a little girl with a pure, gullible heart ensconced in an extremely attractive young woman's body.

Two

After the love accident, Giang Thanh became taciturn, but when she needed to speak, she stubbornly and loudly kept her opinions, and could not hold back a fierce and strong reaction. At the end of the year, in December 1974, she graduated with distinction from the theater school, and at the age of nineteen, Giang Thanh volunteered to go to B (the Southern Battlefield) with a single aim: so that the family would be *"removed from the previous class category"* due to having a daughter volunteering to go South. The father, whose citizenship was restored, replaced his mother to look after the temple, now classified as a center of cultural activities. But the main reason was for her younger sister, Huong Tho, born in 1957, to be able to enroll in the university and join the Ho Chi Minh Communist Youth Union. Then, with time, she would inevitably become an "object for party recruitment."

"The Van Cong delegation was sent to B in the beginning of 1975 after the campaign to capture Phuoc Long was completed in December of 1974. The transportation route called "Ho Chi Minh Trail" was now a two-way highway running along the eastern slopes of Truong Son, deeply hidden in the Southern land, with no more "Socialist Line" located to the west in the territory of Laos and Cambodia in the '60s-'70s."

Giang Thanh was filled with the emotions of those who participated in a decisive period of the nation's history. More specifically, the family situation had been stabilized due to nearly ten years of selfless efforts to take care of her grandmother, father and two younger siblings. She left her salary books, food stamps, rice vouchers, and other groceries to her father with the instructions: "I will go to B on this trip without any incident, waiting for the liberation of the South when I will come back and visit you and my two young sisters. I hope grandma is still alive and healthy until that day. When you receive my salary, don't spend it all. Remember to leave a few dongs a month so that later the family can have a small reserve for the two of my sisters."

She didn't think that she was just twenty, and that the life ahead of her was still full of unforeseen, unexpected contingencies. At the time of her departure, her father appeared as a man totally subdued and broken by the circumstances, and now, despite efforts to recover, had become powerless. He looked at his daughter, in her olive khaki clothes and ragged hat, and a checkered shawl around her neck, with unresponsive eyes. He remembered a very long time ago when he also once wore a uniform–that of another army. The military he had belonged to was once powerful and famous around the world, but finally lost the battle to this country and all ability to repeat the glory. He felt strange to his own daughter. He felt unfamiliar with the life he had been living, that he had endured and shared for many decades. He kissed his daughter on the cheek. The act of affection had not been performed for a long time, nor has anyone seen it repeated or expressed. Giang Thanh realized, and felt very realistically, the sad part in the father's eyes about a vague, yet also very specific, impression about this B trip that would not exactly be a joyful event like everyone around her was jubilantly extoling."

The Zil convoy carried the crew across the Ben Hai River into the territory of Quang Tri province, Gio Linh commune, the land that had been an inspiration for the eloquent song by an artist before 1954 that was the idol of the lovers of patriotic music and the heroic fighting of the two North / South – the fight to defend the country that started on the night of December 19, 1946 in Hanoi; Hai Phong with the Tu Ve Thanh with young hair, in white shirts, with someone even wearing a felt hat when fighting. The young people, university students, high school students–even people of the vagabond type–had used their bodies to block the machine guns of the French Expeditionary Corps. This was the very battle that writers and poets described with each word burning hot and bright red, including Tran Huyen Tran: *'Fired! Gun fired! Hai Phong spits blood into the ocean.'* Chinh Huu, similarly, etched his words into history with, *'I remember the night when the sky was on fire. The whole city was burning behind.'* Along with these majestic verses, a particular song by Pham Duy, the Gio Linh Mother, painted a fierce and tragic situation: *'An old mother goes to take her child's head. In the distance, the temple bell rings.'"*

At the year-end party, on the occasion of the 1974 to 1975 Lunar New Year, Giang Thanh and her friends in the dance group described, urged, and praised the second resistance war. It was now coming to an end with a glorious victory expressed in the the songs: *"Uncle is joining us on the march", "Truong Son Dong / Truong Son Tay"*. But unlike the expectations of the dance troupe, on the sand beach of Diem Ha Nam Hamlet, amid the rumbling sound of waves, the army troops holding the artillery positions and the people attending the party did not seem excited participating in a fun night organized from the day the group set foot in the South."

The next morning, Giang Thanh asked a question to the political commissar of the army unit: *"Why didn't our army comrades seem excited when we sang? And the masses didn't seem that way, either?"*

"How can you be excited, Miss? There are only so many left of Division 308! In 1972, when you came here, you'd only break your bones after a few minutes standing on the ground. Not only our side but the puppet soldiers also suffered the same fate. No one could avoid this–both sides took bombs and fire. Bullets and bombs were stamped down regardless of which side, on the ground, while the positions were a few meters apart. The battle in September 1972 was like rice and husk mixed together. How can we tell which bullets were from the enemy and which from our side? Do you see that over there?"

Giang Thanh looked out into the distance, to the west, behind the sand dunes, scattered bamboo ramparts. She saw mounds of dirt and collapsed structures. That was Quang Tri City, and those mounds used to be an ancient brick citadel built two hundred years ago like the gates used to enter Hanoi!

Giang Thanh went south with a heavy heart. The vague feeling she had from the moment she left now became more specific looking at the villages she passed through. And even more than that, she had a fluttering premonition about something of her own misfortune–that some kind of disaster was awaiting.

Leaving Quang Tri, the delegation followed a communications line protected and escorted by a reconnaissance company through military bases, areas occupied and encroached by the liberation army since the years of the General Offensive in 1972, or after the 1973 Paris Agreement, and in the year 1974. The localities, where the residents had different accents and use of words, had strange names such as Ba Long, Cua, Ty, Tieu, Bac, and Dac villages. Nevertheless, all these places shared the same scenery: These were the desolate towns and villages in the middle of misty mountains, or on arid grassy hills. However, everywhere she heard words of joy and excitement: Now it's *"peace,"* not like a few years ago, *"when there were still Americans"* and you can't sleep on the ground because of *"shelling from the Liberation Front!" "Peace is at hand."*

"'No more Americans,'" but how come you can't see towns and cities? And why did this *"war of liberation"* continue? And where were the *"people of the South trapped under the yoke of the Americans and the Puppet Regime,"* awaiting liberation from the North!?" Silent questions appeared in Giang Thanh's mind at the same time with the nostalgia for her hometown, where her sisters were, along with the melancholy eyes of her father.

It was not until mid-March that the delegation was informed of the good news: The Central Highlands Army Corps had liberated Buon Ma Thuot, but because the situation there was still complicated, the performing group was not allowed to perform yet, although the soldiers and people were excitedly waiting to welcome them.

To make this source of joy come true, the delegation was given fresh food and high-class canned food branded "ARVN Army Provision Service" with the image of a soldier holding a gun (USA) and the Yellow Flag with Three Red Stripes. The group boarded military vehicles bigger and stronger than the Zil (made in China) and continued to go south at an urgent speed until the end of March to enter a city as beautiful as in Western pictures: Da Lat. And Giang Thanh and all the members of the delegation could not help but cry out in amazement at the large gate of a majestic barracks spreading across the lofty hills: the Vietnam National Military School.

The singing and dancing team was arranged to sleep in

separate rooms, with each room comprised of two iron beds, mattresses, and pure white linens arranged at right angles. "These bedrooms belong to the puppet cadets. They are trained like this to oppress and kill people!"

The commissar tried to find an (appropriate) explanation for the comfortable, neat and clean setting of the barracks, which although the occupants of the room must have left in an emergency, the floor still had a clean shine, making people afraid to soil it.

But the explanation–even though it was deliberately forced, and the speaker did not believe what he said himself–was no longer effective when the team was ordered to clean up the spoils in the library. The large piles of books with leather spines and golden letters lined up in the hall were solemnly silent: The inner strength of wisdom as expressed in the words of the people who had built civilization and human culture. Those who study and read these books just cannot be professional murderers, eating human liver and drinking human blood, or throwing babies into the fire?! Giang Thanh nurtured a very specific concept. And she really sank into a sense of guilt–the crime of destruction, with the blood and human flesh she had ravaged and soaked in with her own hands–when she and her companions were ordered to burn the library's volumes.

The fire flared up... Her friends joked, bursting with joy throwing the books into the fire... *Now these books! Now these books!... Your mother's grave books... Read them to your heart's content... study hard to slaughter the people!* Giang Thanh heard the pain on her skin. It was as if she was being burned alive with these books. She tried to hide the biggest, thickest, most beautiful books, with covers printed in the classic Roman typeface, with golden engravings. She had a feeling of consolation as if she had saved people - the people who were honest, good, and noble.

On the party night, Giang Thanh drank everything her friends brought. Wine No. 7 was pungent; Johnny Walker was fragrant with barley; Champagne bottles were opened with a bang and golden foam came spurting out. *Red wine, like blood... Wine... Wine...* Grandpa, grandma, the French man named Pha (as heard in the stories they used to tell), and the father wearing a jacket with many pockets, a rough camisole (only worn in the house during the cold season). *"The wine is all here!"* Giang Thanh soaked it into her body as if she was receiving a familiar kind of water, the blood of her father, her mother, of the past, when she was still imperious, beautiful, and elegant. When her mother was still alive.

She drank it down as if she swallowed the same miserable, dangerous childhood, getting up in the early morning and awakened alone in the cold night. From the age of fourteen alone, she had overcome poverty to support her father and younger sisters. Giang Thanh drank the wine of victory mixed with her tears. She laughed heartily, and said to Son in slurred words: *"You are an asshole. I love you the most, but I also despise you the most. Damn your forefathers. You had nothing to gain from sleeping with Diem like that, but you lost me completely. I didn't suffer at all, but only regretted that I once loved you. If I wanted to take revenge on you, I would kill you right away but I need not do it. My mother was killed, so I am afraid of being a murderer, no, I'm not afraid of you. I dare you to hit me like last year when I still loved you, so I had endured you!"* She spit and splashed the wine on Son's face, that same boy who had been with her for seven years at the theater school sharing a dear friendship–and then also the very one that helped her understand the betrayal of trivial love.

Giang Thanh did not know how she had returned to her sleeping place, and with whom. In the middle of the night, she woke up with a burning sensation in her genitals. She reached down and touched her crotch. It was wet with blood, and the mucus had dried on the hairs.

Giang Thanh had to go out before the meeting of the party secretary to answer about the crime of depravity that had begun to show concrete evidence with a pregnancy that became more and more pronounced. But she was not a humdrum type. Her face hardened, her voice sounded like broken jade, she said to the secretariat: "I'm not the wretched, depraved, crazy type of person. I am a revolutionary soldier. As a superior actor of the theater troupe, I went to the South to encourage the soldiers in the liberation of the South. That night, the night of jubilee drinking, everyone was drunk, not just me. Maybe I was drunk the worst. The next day when I asked for a gynecological examination, the doctor confirmed that I was raped, the medical evidence was still there, and I had reported the matter to the secretariat. If I did this surreptitiously, why should I go to report it? No one is stupid enough to report her own stealth! And I also asked to see a gynecologist twice later to ask the doctor to have an abortion. Today, I still have that intention. Even if the abortion leads to infection or bleeding and death, I will not refuse. I will sign a paper now to affirm this decision. The secretariat should have found that bastard, forced him to be disciplined, demoted him, expelled him from the ranks of the party members. Are Communist Party members like that? Where is the revolutionary morality Uncle Ho had taught you scoundrels? (she intentionally used the words '*you scoundrels*'). What kind of party members took off their drunk comrades' pants and raped them!?"

Her eyes were wide open, her voice was loud. So much anger and resentment (for the past five months, due to many reasons...) had exploded without concealment.

The secretariat finally came up with a solution: All the

male group members had to do self-examination to find the culprit. The examination led to easy results with three confessors, including the deputy secretary and the guy named Son. All the *"three perpetrators"* agreed to admit their fault, and asked to be redeemed by an official wedding with Giang Thanh, hosted by the secretariat. But no one could predict the outcome. Giang Thanh smiled scornfully, pointing at the faces of the three *"culprits"* with words like knives cutting stones: "Guys, look at your faces. A person like me has to call you guys husbands? The pregnancy in my womb has already been a disgrace. Marrying you guys, I'd have to endure that shame for the rest of my life."

She changed her voice: "I don't need any one of you to bear the brunt of the misery caused by one of the three of you now. But I also knew who it was." She looked at the man named Son, firmly stating, "You have humiliated me twice. Now you think that through this "admission," you will be tied to me. Don't try! I will abort this pregnancy, or if I let it live, I'd never let you accept the baby in my belly as your child. My child doesn't have the kind of vile, cowardly father like you!"

The guy named Son fell to the ground and lamented: "I bow to you, I beg you to keep the child. It's *our* child. After all, we had had an engagement ceremony before, we were just not married yet. It's fine if you don't let me take it, but please don't give it up. Last night I had a very clear dream about it–a daughter, exactly like the one my sister had let suffocate to death in the shelter bunker the year before in Thai Binh."

"Who is husband-and-wife with you? If I keep the baby, it's because it came from my belly. You're an asshole who doesn't deserve to be its father." Giang Thanh's voice was still firm, but with a hint of bitterness and boredom, not entirely with the anger at the beginning of the meeting.

At the end of 1975, on December 28, exactly nine months and ten days after the drunkenness spell in the Da Lat Academy, Giang Thanh gave birth to a baby girl at the infirmary run by a Chinese midwife, named Luong, on Hai Ba Trung Street, at the junction with Tran Quang Khai Street and Tran Nhat Duat Street. Here was a house that Uong Dai Dung had bought and given to his eighth concubine in 1915, sixty years ago, also in the Year of the Cat.

Three

Giang Thanh refused the privileges reserved for an artist promoted to the level of *"Superior Artist"* if she agreed to return to Hanoi with the dance troupe. She applied to stay in Saigon, enrolled in the National School of Music, now converted to become the No. 2 School of Music and Art, in the Director class, knowing that a performer only has one period and one specific field–singing, dancing, film, or drama–and will be limited by age, the environment, and the professional requirements (no matter how excellent the talent, how skillful the technique, she won't last long in this profession). But it's not the same with the role of a director. With the advancement of age, a director becomes more stable and mature. And yet, she had been subjected to criticism, reproach, even cruelty: *"She wanted to stay in Saigon because she was infected with the smell of leftover butter and milk left behind by the puppets. That type of gal would only end up lying on her back to sell her body to feed her mouth. That Son was begging in front of the group like that, but she even kicked the boy like a dog–how could she love anyone? That little child of hers would end up in an orphanage so her mother could have her way of sleeping around."*

To these not-so-good *"prophecies,"* she replied

uncompromisingly: *"In the North, at fourteen years old, I could still support my family bearing the American bombs; today, you guys are lying and sneering, but one of these days you will run clinging to the hem of my pants to ask for favors."* She had not exaggerated with empty words because she already had a plan, actually a decision, with two abilities to her advantage: A radiant beauty that projects itself naturally, and an innate intelligence coming from her keen intuition, which helped her see other people's activities, words, and ideas from the very time they started. And more than anyone else, she knew herself very well so that she was very confident, and at the same time, she knew how to maintain a clear mind because she had gone through suffering without getting drowned. But she was also ready to talk back harshly and severely, responding with accuracy every word and sentence from the opponent. One thing for sure, Giang Thanh was not afraid or easily discouraged.

The South in general, and Saigon in particular, after April 30, 1975, fell into a strange and tragic situation after more than a hundred years since its formation, resulting in a unique and exceptional scene. The tragic situation was created by the South Vietnamese themselves, and implemented through a life-changing reversal, so it became terrible. Though called *"the national liberation revolution,"* in fashionable political parlance, few people were willing to use that phrase when they compared it with the realities of *"before the liberation."* The yellow buses running on Gia Dinh streets, and the green ones traversing the inner city of Saigon, had quickly become legends of the past. The houses and shops on Le Loi, Tu Do, and Le Thanh Ton Streets displayed a sad and pitiful look, the way a girl wearing trendy, expensive clothes of the day before suddenly changed into a white folksy shirt, locally-spun black pants, and plastic sandals made in Chợ Lớn–the kind of new reality accurately described by poet Hoàng Cầm as, *"Whiskered sandals, braided hair black pants, white shirt, maid appearance."* The southerners were both surprised and amused by the "portrait of the liberator." The victor was just an awkward opponent, manipulating a U.S.-branded personal shovel in hand, bewilderedly walking in front of the city hall, confusedly looking up at the tall buildings with praises, like, *"Terrifying!"* And the maid had now become the family's savior with the assurance of an alderman: *"Don't be afraid of anyone, just move down to the garage to live; I am now the owner of this house, belonging to the city commando team, in charge of the women of Phú Nhận district ("Nhận" instead of "Nhuận")*. The Saigonese had to express all their thoughts and feelings in the ubiquitous word *"good"* with the way of saying *"having been taught"* after many nights of neighborhood meetings, reviews, votes, reports on the achievements in labor emulation, increased production: *"Report to cadre. I have been good in work, achieved and exceeded the target sent down by high-ups."* From the old lady selling snail vermicelli in Phu Nhuan market to the old rickshaw driver, the young conductor of a transport cab, all the way to the little waiter at a publicly run "phở" eatery. Everyone had the same report with content that they had learned by heart. Every night from 8 to 11 o'clock, with the job done, go to bed so that in the morning at six o'clock they go to the cultural park to exercise according to the new cultural and civilized lifestyle. And as consolation, the people of Saigon appeased their misfortunes through mocking sentences, including, *"Down with Thieu-Ky, you have everything. Hooray Ho Chi Minh, you have to queue to buy a nail."* Everyone was equal in a miserable, pitiable situation through an economic and social mechanism called *"the regime of total subsidy."*

Giang Thanh could not escape the plight of poverty on account of the revolutionary glory she had contributed to the achievement. The fixed salary of a student at the School of Music and Art could not help her support herself, let alone to feed baby Thanh Giang. She named her child by reversing her own name to show her determination–it was *her* own child. And hers alone. Since little Thanh Giang had only been registered as an illegitimate child because she had no marriage certificate, the girl was not called the child of the new regime, the Socialist regime. The regime that had put an end to the phenomenon of people exploiting people. Thanh Giang was not counted in her mother's salary. Therefore, Giang Thanh strived to raise her daughter by herself.

She was given the job of waitress running the night shift at Bat Dat restaurant for two nights. The third night, the manager came to her while she was putting on her uniform before the shift: "You are so beautiful, so fragrant." He sucked in his wide nostrils to confirm that he was imbued with the scent of the girl's flesh. Giang Thanh stopped putting on her shirt and looked at the manager. Misunderstanding her silence, he moved forward: "You don't have to waste your time serving the tables anymore. Stop wearing this uniform starting tonight. Go to my room, the management room, on the eighth floor, the one with the goldfish tank in front."

"If I don't wear it, I cloak it on your head, OK?! You got the wrong person, scoundrel!"

Giang Thanh put the cloak on the manager's head. Then she turned and walked away. She also got into similar *"incidents"* at a few other restaurants, or was warned by the managers' wives to tear up *"the Tonkinese girl as white as a cross-breed, as beautiful as Thanh Nga, Mong Tuyen."* In the end, she chose to wash dishes at Nam Do Hotel, transformed into a state-owned restaurant, the official reception venue for the central troupes coming to Saigon to perform.

No one knew that a talented drama actress, folk dance and song performer, and choreographer was also a kitchen assistant (on weekend nights) working shifts with tall piles of soiled dishes, washing sticky food with bare hands using locally produced soap. But Giang Thanh never complained. She said out loud to herself: *"This is nothing compared to running to escape the American bombings from Mai Dich to Ha Dong on an empty stomach!"* She also had the joy of asking the management to take out a part of her salary for two fried chickens to treat her classmates. *"Eat them, guys. This is from my salary, not from anyone else. Eat up, I haven't been able to treat you to a decent meal from the day we started school."* It was also because she was inherently playful and loved to take care of others, because she understood the meaning of happiness, being loved, and showing love to others.

"Comrade student Giang Thanh, please report to the group from where you got the two roasted chickens to treat to the students in the directing class. Those two chickens were worth more than half of the student's base salary. Where did they come from–if not from illicit relations!?"

For a moment, Giang Thanh choked with frustration because she couldn't imagine that a good conduct would lead to this terrible result. Suppressing her indignation, she counterattacked, "Where did that come from? Are you implying that I worked as a call girl to have money for those chickens? I'm not that cheap! If I want to be a call girl, I know the way down to the Ben Nghe Hotel to go to foreign customers with large sums of money, more than my whole yearly salary. And if you want to know why I have those chickens, go and ask Nam Do. Last Saturday night they were entertaining the Hong Ha dance troupe from outside Hanoi, after performing at the Bong Sen music venue. But if I had to turn myself into a prostitute, you comrades should also be ashamed along with me. A performer that volunteered to go B had to sell her body after the South was liberated. Who should be more ashamed than who!? Who was more painful than who!? As a result of the revolution leading to the national liberation and unification of the country, the warrior had to sell her body to feed her mouth–what is the logic of *that*? And that piece of chicken was not only for me, but also for the mouths of the comrades who are sitting here presiding over this review. Judge me! Criticize me! Who has the right to criticize whom? What to review and critique!?"

Giang Thanh pushed the atmosphere of the review into a dark, damning tragedy. When she recalled it later, she regretted that she had not said it better, more bitingly: *"Had I decided to speak up, I'd send you all to hell."* In the end, Giang Thanh decided to leave Nam Do Restaurant to carry fish at Cau Ong Lanh market with a curse of herself: *"Mother's grave to you, grandma sacrifice my body here to raise my child to see if anyone dares touch it, cajole it or force it!"* Every night, she sneaked up at one o'clock in the morning, tucked in the mosquito net to put her child to sleep, rode her bike down to the fish stall on the corner of Co Giang Street and Nguyen Thai Hoc Street. Having a tall, sturdy body, Giang Thanh ran without difficulty with a basket of fish on her head, only worrying about the brine running down her hair, wetting her face, and sullying her with a strong fishy smell. Coming back at four o'clock in the morning, she washed her hair and bathed to remove the odors from her hair and skin.

Fortunately, the weather in the South was always hot, so she didn't have to suffer the cold, but soaking in water for an hour in the early morning for a long time later caused sinusitis, making her voice hoarse, losing its clear timbre. In return, the miserable situation forged Giang Thanh's will more persistently, making her sympathize more easily with the plight of people (herself actually). She staged Bertolt Brecht's play, T*he Courageous Mother and Her Children*, to denounce the crimes of the Fascists and the capitalists causing a war that persecuted innocent people, and played the role of a mother so masterfully that no one could match her. In fact, she just needed to externalize the pain of herself and of the women in the Uong family on stage.

The play was actually adapted from Bertolt Brecht's original work by the ideological and cultural commissioner in the school's secretariat, Le Đau. Đau came from Thanh Hoa where there were similes (not just folk songs and proverbs of this locality to disparage and ridicule other localities) showing enough personality about the people and affairs of the land that had given rise to the bloody wars lasting from the 16th and 17th centuries. The Southern/Northern dynasties had for 60 years, while the Trinh/Nguyen had for more than a hundred years, been fighting fiercely around this area on both sides of the Ngang Pass. *"Thanh Hoa eats pennyworth, breaks the railroad tracks!"* The Thanh Hoa people were really proud of their resilient, strong, and destructive nature. The expression *"Kicking the ball like Thanh Hoa!"* is a prime example of their ethos, referencing the technique of kicking a soccer ball to win whatever the cost. Thanh Hoa not only had glory in language, poetry, and singing, but in fact, Colonel Đang Vu Nam had defeated the armies of Charton and Le Page on Route 4 (1953), captured two senior commanders alive on the battlefield, and completely destroyed an inter-army mobile corps of the French army in an ingenious and skillful campaign of guerrilla tactics leading to the level of the whole battlefield.

Thanh Hoa was a safe zone during the war of 1946-1954, and was also the locality that led the battle of *"To Kho"* against landlords, breaking down the thousand-year-old bamboo ramparts protecting the villages of the homeland, pinning down the cries and laments of thousands of people suffering and falling down. Đau went South with an affirmation: *"Fuck them! Can Tho, Gia Dinh are not only reserved to the Southerners. Whoever is strong will take it."* Đau did not translate the play just due to his translator's job, but as he said to Giang Thanh, *"I translated this play for you. You'll make it into a worthwhile drama different from their uncouth plays. The kind of communist soldier like Paven (The Communist youth character in a Russian revolutionary novel) shovels snow to make revolution! With this, you'll go on a big stage like that of the central Moscow troupe."*

While rehearsing, even though he had no sympathy for Đau, Giang Thanh also had to say to herself: "This old monster is really admirable, the dialogue of Bertolt Brecht that he translated sounds like in a play by Luu Quang Vu."

For Giang Thanh's thirtieth birthday, in 1985, despite being still in the general subsidy period with numerous common difficulties (because all the assets and treasures confiscated from the South had to be paid back to Russia, China, and to compensate for the privations the North had to suffer since 1945). But Saigon still could not be *"as poor"* as Hanoi, Hai Phong, so Đau was able to acquire a bouquet of thirty Brigitte roses appraised by the guests as *"more beautiful than the bouquet Uncle Ton sent to the Politburo out there,"* and a birthday cake *"as big as the baseplate of a Chinese 82 mortar."* No one knew where the old *"Đau Fucking"* could find something like that!

Đau acquired the accolade *"Fuck"* because he always started sentences with *"I don't fucking need"* or *"We don't fucking understand"* in all transactions. Even when talking to the secretary of the cultural ministry, he blurted, "Report to you...I *'fucking'* don't think the Southerners could *'fucking'* do anything to us!" The secretary, who perfectly summed up both the *"people's and party's character,"* replied: *"That shows you don't 'fucking' understand them at all."*

In the literal sense, Đau couldn't help but *"fuck"* even for a day as he described himself: "I don't know how I'm always messing around like this. Fucking damn it, if I'm a woman, I'd have to have an abortion once a day!" Đau did not exaggerate about himself, for he could not have described it more accurately.

In Saigon after 1975 with most Southern men going to concentration camps and North Vietnamese soldiers dying scattered along Truong Son, many women, educated or not, had nothing to make a living besides their own bodies. People like Đau with the bad habit of *"fucking"* were not an obstacle, but were even sometimes *"praised."*

In front of Đau's house, there were always girls waiting: *"He told me, whenever there is no customer, no place to eat or sleep, come by here."* But Đau was not only *"plenty"* with the *"fucking"* custom, he also was *"plenty"* in all other things. When you eat it, make it worthwhile. To bite the meat, you must take it to the teeth. He would say, "I never *"fucking"* touch those vegetables, squashes, eggplants... Waste my time... shitting!"

Đau did not exaggerate. Indeed, he never put any vegetables, squash, or beans in his mouth. Eggs were his vegetables. Meat was his rice. The pussy was his charm! *"You shout so aggressively, you've owned such a treasure of learning, why not write a book? Could it be that your head and heart only contain such trivial things?"* Some people asked him these questions with the intention of pushing him to a corner. Đau quickly grasped the opponent's intentions, spitting out the saliva-soaked cigarette butts to remark, *"My head...I just think about it, and my life is already a complete masterwork. No need to add another word. As for the heart... Fucking damn it, my heart belongs to the glorious Party... Heh...heh!"*

Đau looked menacingly at the other side behind his thick glasses. With this lifestyle of eating, sleeping and thinking, Đau's head and body were always as hot as a ball of fire, so he could only wear shorts and a short-sleeved shirt twice unbuttoned at the neck. Đậu slept right on the floor, not on a bed or mattress. With such lifestyle, Giang Thanh was a *"target"* that Đau could not ignore. *"Fucking damn it, I have to catch this girl even if you run up into the sky!"* When Đau swore in full words, that signaled an extremely *"urgent"* matter that needed to be attended to.

So, when the time came, Ms. Thuy Hương, Đau's wife, a beautiful woman who specialized in modeling for trade and women's fashion magazines (Dao had brought her to the South after 1975) became a burden. *"If you do modeling, it's a waste of money if you don't take nude photos. Let me ask the cameraman and photographer at our school to come home and make some shots for you."* Huong believed Dau, also because her lover (a professional photographer in Saigon before 1975), made a similar comment. Moreover, she was also interested in participating in the *"advanced civilized activities that the Americans and the puppets had previously started and reached a high level of artistry."* And when the photographer was fumbling to fix Thuy Huong's lying down position, Đau broke through the door of the room and rushed in with two neighborhood policemen (even though he had the room key) shouting, *"Oh my God! Oh my God! The most beautiful model in Hanoi! My wife!"* Đau fell to the ground first to allow two police officers to photograph the crime scene. Đau got the house on Nguyen Hue Street with the evidence of *"fault on the wife's part."* The house on the front street before 1975 was the premises of Thang Long Photo Institute, which Thuy Huong had occupied in the name of the Liberation Photography Association.

In the middle of Giang Thanh's birthday party, Đau presented the divorce papers showing the reason: the wife was caught making love on the spot! Giang Thanh was also too tired of a lonely life that someone always inquires into with rude intentions, including, *"Let me be the father of your baby!"* She agreed to marry Đau with a covenant: *"After you marry me, you can sleep with whomever you want (I already know how "bloody greedy" you are). I just ask you not to bring the girls home while I'm away. I don't want my girl to see that filth! When my child grows up, and goes abroad to study, I'll immediately join a nunnery.*

"What's the big deal! I can take care of it. You don't fucking have to tell me!" Đau made the boisterous commitment, and turned around to hide a smile. This baby is so sharp, can't fucking play around with her!

Having been officially married for a week, Giang Thanh confirmed her suspicion: Đau's loud-mouthed *"fucking"* show off was only meant to conceal the truth. He was incapable of fulfilling his *"sexual duty as a husband,"* or to become a father in the normal sense. Đau excused his flaws with a simple smile, chiming *"I only have a strong mouth, don't you mind!"* But it was when Đau revealed this poor weakness with a very rare, childish smile that Giang Thanh's heart calmed down. She proffered comforting words, such as, *"It doesn't matter that much, as long as Dad loves and protects me and my child. Dad just "doesn't" go fucking where he wants to be, don't bring the girls home, and don't cast diseases onto yourself–that would only make yourself miserable, and bring shame on me.*

To repay the generous sympathy of his wife, the next day Đau took the basket to the market in a joyful manner, a wide smile stretched to his ears. *"I went to the market to cook for you and your child."* For the first time, Đau bought vegetables, beans, and tubers. Đau proudly explained to the shopkeeper, "I bought these to cook soup for her." It was also the first time he didn't use the word *"fucking"* in his speech. And Giang Thanh was really touched when Đau fumbled bringing a bowl of soup to mother and child. He admitted, *"I only knew how to prepare cocktails my whole life. This is the first time I have to be a "househusband" to serve you and your child."* Đau laughed excitedly and sat down with baby Thanh Giang. *Let Daddy feed you.* Giang Thanh smiled happily with her eyes, thinking to herself, *"Well, even if he showed any mess-up, I'd just have to accommodate for the sake of my family and the country. I'm just hoping to be at peace like this."*

But Đau's (well-intentioned) efforts were shaken after the end of an extremely satisfying love affair (because he was no more responsible, and was not bound by the obligation of being a husband) with female artist Xuan Hong. She was a literary, poetic, and musical star from Hanoi to perform in the city named after Uncle. Xuan lit a Đien Bien cigarette wrapped in aluminum foil (the cigarette was the most advanced type produced by Hanoi). *"Throw it away my dear. Take this three numbers kind (Imported Tobacco, Brand 555). Sleeping with you and smoking this peasant thing brought in from Hanoi amounts to no less than cursing you."* Actually Đau just wanted to demonstrate the stylishness of the *"Saigon people to show off to the people from out there"* without the intention of playing down the female artist. But Xuân Hong was not to be sneered at, boldly claiming, "Mother's grave to your whole family. Three numbers and what not. Haven't you eaten shrimp paste with dog meat in your mouth, or smoked water pipes for decades? Now that you have just been attending to a slut pregnant out of wedlock as a housekeeper, carrying the potty for her, and you've already forgotten the *"pure revolutionary character"* of ideological culture cadres as you often taught us in class. Do you know how she described you?

With a surge in enthusiasm, Đau sat up and asked, "What did she say?"

"She said you're a castrated rooster, nothing but the mouth!"

Đau could ignore many things, but because the female singer was very smart, she knew how to hit the opponent's very *"vital nerve."* "Is that what she said?" Đau impertinently demanded, his face swelling crimson as if he were sitting on the fire.

"Would anyone know if she hadn't said it? Even the scene when you carried the potty for her and her daughter." Đau weakly protested.

"Come on now, watch your mouth!"

The lady sneered, "You tell yourselves to keep your mouth shut, not anyone else. Strange indeed, how can someone like you be so easily fooled? I had thought you were as tall as a mountain. Who'd have believed you're just an earthen ball?"

Xuan Hong knew how to lift up and throw down. Đau was cranky and bemoaned, "No fucking one can lead me on! I'm not the type of person who crawls under the bed screaming and puts his butt out for someone else to kick his ass. Whoever is good enough to *"screw"* me, I'm soft out of compassion, that's all."

Xuan Hong turned to the second *"fatal"* issue: "How many gold taels has she spent since marrying you?"

The blow was very effective. Đau faltered, "What does that have to do with you?"

The lady smiled faintly. "It has nothing to do with me, but just to let you know, all the Hanoi people are talking about *"Fucking Đau"* playing ruffian to get Thuy Huong's house, and is now going to sacrifice himself to Giang Thanh to gain the reputation of being a so-called husband. Damn, people like me just wanted to be a bride to my father's *"Great Magnificent Le Family."* Your daddy is not a kid, a boy, or a maid carrying a basket to market to serve the mother and daughter, clean up dog shit, and feed cats. Being married to my daddy, a literary advisor, I'd be awarded the literary prize of the Writers Association at once. Daddy is a real master, right!"

Đau tucked his shirt in his pants; the cigarette in his mouth was shivering, wet. "Fuck you all," he quietly protested.

"Hey, if you want to curse, go home and do it. I'm not a trash can for you to dump all your shit," Xuan Hong hissed.

Đau barked, determinedly, "You'll soon know my turn!"

"What the fuck are you to know and don't know!"

Xuan Hong had spilled the provocative glass of water. Angrily running down the stairs, Đau muttered, "Fuck you! Fuck you all!"

But when Đau stepped into the house, Giang Thanh took action first. Cups, plates, crockery, porcelain, mirrors, glass cabinets, windows, and dressing tables had all become a jagged pile of rubble that filled the house. She said, rather succinctly, "Bastard. I've commanded your life on to you from the first day. You have the right to go "fuck around," but not to humiliate me. That bitch Xuan Hong has gone all over the place, spreading the news that I married you just to take over the house you had stolen, framing the scene of Thuy Huong sleeping with a photographer. They said I married you because of the gold. Even if a dog would cringe at your rotten dick, your face is as evil as a mastiff. Which house, which gold, huh?!"

Giang Thanh had become an *"enemy"* for showing Dau's fatal and irreversible *"defects."* But even though she was a brave woman who has been forged by hardships, she still retained the genuine and sensitive mind of an artist coming from a prestigious family and a pure culture. She just couldn't imagine and anticipate the vile and despicable situations that had caused her anger. And so after wreaking havoc and seeing Dau silently clean up, showing patience and regrets, (all the broken items were piled up into two large dumps that Dau tried his best to manage but couldn't move; the broken eyeglasses dangled in one ear, his hair drooping). Giang Thanh felt guilty about her excessive behavior. She laughed softly, scolding, "Move out, good-for-nothing! Just a lying mouth!"

And she almost forgot about Dau's fault, until the next day, when he produced a gold tael and went out to buy replacements for the broken things with a compliment and a smile for assuagement. "Next time, remember to only break the earthenware ones–save the expensive ones!"

"There's no next time. Next time I'll smash your head." She had completely forgotten the accident.

Like a handicap that cannot be changed, even with deliberate effort, Dau repeated the *"fucking around"* achievements not only once but many times, albeit in a wiser, more discreet way with *"objects"* that he considered *"harmless."* He explained to Giang Thanh, "I don't like those women. They can't touch your heels in value. But I want them to know that we out there are better than the puppets in all matters, including the business of bedside achievements!"

Giang Thanh's reply was also *"extremely"*: "I don't know

who *'won'* who! I don't know in what matter you're better than the puppets, but the *'about the bedside business'* you've lost to them for sure. Don't brag to me!"

"Have you *'tested'* them already to know that?"

Giang Thanh quickly became angry, sneering, "I have no time to *'test or text'* at all? I just look at you walking back every time you called it *'to take over the spoils left by the puppets'* to know right away! Is there any *'trophy'* looking for you a second time? Maybe only because of the remaining gold taels you'd brought from the North. But rest assured: As soon as my child got to secondary school, I will leave you right away, because I've found an apartment on Nguyen Trai Street. You can freely go to *'revenge the puppet army, the puppet government'* and pay for the *"depraved products left by the My-Thieu regime.'* I leave you alone with your women. *'Uncle Ho's descendants'* or *'American and Thieu's henchmen'* are no different to me.

The above dialogues ended at the time Giang Thanh presented the divorce papers with the fault resting on *'the husband has committed adultery.'* Dau was dumbfounded and asked the honest question, "How...*how* did you get those papers?"

Giang Thanh slowly, thoroughly, decisively replied, "I forbid you to use *uncle, aunt, brother, sister*...with me from now on. You asked me how I got these papers? So you don't remember the achievements of *'avenge (wife, children) of the puppet army, the puppet government'* you boasted to me? You taught me many things, and I have learned a few things. Would you like to hear those achievements again? I've made a lot of tapes, and they sound very interesting. With the cassette player that you boasted you've recorded the time you had sex with the consort of a puppet minister that had fled to America, leaving her behind in that villa on the way to the airport. Do you still remember the time you were cursing while having sex to get that motherfucker more excited?

"Then auntie…"

"Hey, I said no more *'uncle, aunty!'*"

"Well, then what do you want?" said Đau, decisively.

"I don't want anything. I leave this house without taking a bowl, or a pair of chopsticks from you. One day I invite you to visit my Nguyen Trai house, number… Alley 222. That number is easy to remember."

"You let me go up to your house, and you come down here to visit me. I beg you. I know I've been wrong. It's been almost three years since I lived with you. I can't be without you and the baby. Please understand me. I can't live alone! Dau knelt down and kissed Giang Thanh's feet.

"That's what I say to you privately, no one outside knows it. It's not good to leave one man today and marry another tomorrow. When I get out of the country with my daughter, I'll make a public statement, and then people can think whatever they want. After my child and I moved to Nguyen Trai's house, if you want to come down to eat, just call to let me know in advance, or I would cook at this house if I'm free that day. Let's consider ourselves as a couple separated due to work."

Dau put his face down on Giang Thanh's feet for a long time, expressing gratitude and remorse.

Epilogue

"Well, that's fine, your little sister is truly tough and wise." The listener of the story sighed and spoke as if they were exhausted after a hard journey. *"But in the end, it's not*

the way you might think." "Oh heaven and earth. What else is there now?!" The friend lamented as if seeing a disaster looming before her eyes.

1995

In November, Dau went to Nguyen Trai's house with an elderly Frenchman, with bright white wavy hair pressed close to his noble, stylish head. He used a French language spoken with the correct style that was common at the beginning of the century in Franco-Southern schools throughout Indochina.

"This is a very worthy woman to receive all the best favors, and I am a bad man that does not deserve this noble woman."

"You... Yes, only you have been destined to be placed by her side with all the best fit. I respectfully entrust to you the reward that God always gives to the good-hearted."

Giang Thanh did not fully understand the content of Dau's words, but she understood the meaning of the words *"admirable, respectable, noble"* repeated many times in the sentence, and the solemn attitude of the guest when he heard the word *"Dieu,"* and bent down to hold her hand in an elegant manner.

"I couldn't totally get what you said to him, but I got the gist of it. So who are you? What do you want?"

This was the inspector general of the Michelin car tire maker, Mr. Paul de Lucassan, who came to Vietnam to work with our government to review the management of rubber plantations, to start a joint venture, and open a car tire factory.

"What does the production of car tires and aircraft tires have to do with me?"

"Yes, that's why I brought him here. He had seen the movie *Auntie* a few years ago, the role of the Undying Mother, and offered to meet *"auntie"* for a long-term discussion.

"What is the long term?"

"To marry *'auntie'* and bring you back to France!"

"Are you selling me?"

"No, never. *"Auntie"* understood me wrong. I am a socialist intellectual, a Communist humanist cultural cadre. Now it's your turn. I'd like to wait outside."

Dau proffered his hand politely, humbly. Lucassan tried to express in the simplest of words, his hands on his chest sincerely, affectionately: "Ma'am, I'm too old. Fifty years old, twice divorced. I'm tired. I don't like being an erotic adventurer. I ask for your hand. *Quand, et comment.*"

Giang Thanh faltered. She tried to maximize her ability and the percentage of French hybrid blood in her body: "Mr. Dau, come in here. You tell me about little Thanh Giang."

Dau quickly ran in showing an eager, active posture. "Don't worry about that. I've told Mr. Lucassan in advance. We only take care of the wedding for now. You're responsible for organizing the wedding party. I'll be responsible for the paperwork and visa for you to follow him. You'll go first, do a Catholic ceremony at his family's private parish church, and then she'll be brought over later."

"What's this about going ahead? When?"

"Monday. It's now Wednesday, only a few days left to take care of many things. Saturday and Sunday is the wedding, so invite as many relatives from Hanoi as possible."

"What money to take care of the wedding, the way of running a funeral like that?"

"Money, dollars, dollars. Here, he's given five thousand in advance."

Dau clearly counted each 100 dollar bill in front of Giang Thanh's (future) husband. And Giang Thanh really could not have predicted the incident when Lucassan put a ring with sparkling diamond beads on her finger. She didn't understand why the ring fit her finger–which is bigger than that of the average Vietnamese woman–so she didn't pay attention to Dau's way of addressing her (deliberately with the accolade *"auntie"*). Why did it fit like that?" She turned the ring anxiously.

Dau, being observant, explained right away: "I took the ring you gave back to me last year as a sample, just to let you know how much I love you. This ring is worth twenty-five thousand dollars, the most expensive in the diamond shop at IMEXCO, Nam Ky Khoi Nghia Street.

When the guest and Dau had left, Giang Thanh sat quietly and asked herself: *"Why did he calculate everything in advance?"* She was surprised at her almost passive attitude. But when thinking about the (very specific) future of young Thanh Giang when she could go out of the country to study abroad, she seemed to have received a strong power–this helped her regain her wisdom and realism. She picked up the phone and proceeded to speak when she heard a voice on the other end: "Is that Mr. Dau? I want to ask you a few things. Who's the master of ceremony? What are the legal conditions, such as the management, inheritance, dowry? Sure, five thousand US dollars and a diamond ring is a big amount of money, but my body and my child's life can't be paid with such money and property. As for my house, jewelry, and child, who will take care of those for me when I leave the country?"

Dau's voice showed firm confidence: "I'll take care of everything. I have taken care of all the papers, civil status, marriage certificate, management conditions, and inheritance.

Even the safe at the bank for you to register your property, the title of your house…"

"Who will take care of my daughter on the day I leave to give her back to me later?" Giang Thanh asked fiercely.

Dau replied with steely determination: "I know she's not even twenty years old, so I have to hasten the wedding before her birthday. She was born on the 28th of next month, December 28th."

Putting down the phone, Giang Thanh returned to the question: *"Why did he figure everything out in the first place? Well, let my child be happy, being out of this wretched country."* Giang Thanh stood up and held a bottle of Johny Walker with the blue label–her habit from the day she began living alone. She looked up at the calendar, flipped to Monday, November 28, and added, "I'm out of here next week. Really?!"

***

After getting off the express train from Paris at Gare de Lyon, Giang Thanh completely lost her idea of time and of France when the Lucassan family car picked her up, left the plains, headed for the mountains to the west, and started up the steep mountain pass. *"This is the Michelin factory. This is the main street, Montlosier. That over there is the church of Notre Dame de Clermont-Ferrand,"* Lucassan explained kindly, slowly pointing to the large block, the black cathedral. *"All the houses, the name of this area belong to the mountains. Tous sont sur des dômes. Tu sais."* Lucassan intimately held the hand of his newlywed wife, kissed her rounded fingers, biting lightly on the tip of her nails: *"Toi. Tu es aussi un dôme. Non, la rivière, pan–pan en montant des montagnes."*

The car stopped in front of a castle built against a cliff, surrounded by a vast expanse of clearing, with tall reeds undulating under the bitter wind of winter. Lucassan pointed to a uneven space with black blocks. "That is the cemetery of the De Lucassan family, those who died in the 11th Century on *"croisade."* Tu sais. *'La Croisade pour défendre Le Royame de Dieu.'"*

Giang Thanh wanted to laugh at the situation, the ongoing story with the man she called husband. She was not afraid, not at all; yet, it felt strange. She felt indifferent. If she could give everything in the world, including her body, to hold her baby in her arms just once. Right now! She certainly would not hesitate to agree.

After nearly a month living in a foreign country, for the first time Giang Thanh regained her dynamism on a day near Christmas Day–Friday the 22nd. It was very cold, and the hill was frozen white in the morning, with only a little sunshine in the afternoon. But it was a happy day because she was about to hear her daughter's voice from her homeland, halfway around the world. Giang Thanh followed her husband down Clermont-Ferrand Street to make a phone call to Thanh Giang. "That is a statue of Vercingétoric, the ancestor of the Gauls." Lucassan pointed to a majestic equestrian statue.

"That over there is Blaise Pascal, the superb French thinker and scientist." He showed reverence and admiration as he circled the flower garden where the statue of a man standing in a contemplative mood was positioned. But all of them were inanimate objects, meaningless to Giang Thanh, because she was nervous and anxious in the wait that she seemed to be about to receive, witnessing a miracle. Giang Thanh held her breath, nervously watching the dialogue between Lucassan and the postal worker as he struggled with a large notebook showing a list of international switchboards. "Impossible. Impossible. Quel est la cité de Ho."

And she broke into ecstasy when the postal worker handed

her the phone with a sigh showing success. "*Tiens, lui voilà.* I'm...here's your mom."

Giang Thanh burst into tears upon hearing the voice from the other side of the world. "Mom...mother...You shouldn't cry...I'm safe. I just need some money to treat my friend for my upcoming birthday. Mom, rest assured, I'm fine. No, I didn't ask him. I don't want to see him...I'm just asking you..."

Giang Thanh panicked and did not understand what happened between her and Dau.

"Listen, I have no reservations about you, everything's yours, but before leaving the country I authorized him because you were not yet twenty years old. Yes, yes I understand you are about to turn twenty. I will come back to you as soon as I finish the guarantee papers...Yes, yes, I'll call you back on your birthday...I miss you...Vietnam is seven hours ahead in time. I know how to call you..."

Giang Thanh was confused between answering and asking, she did not ask why her daughter had any disagreement with Dau. She lost her composure and clarity when thinking about the situation of a lonely child in her hometown–the situation she herself had had to endure since childhood. She felt sorry for her child because the pain of separation devastated her greater than any disaster she had ever encountered. Even more terrifying, Giang Thanh felt the reality of painful parting.

The Christmas holidays for Giang Thanh were like torture, as the weight of time was like a rock that did not move. She floated around, laughed, ate. Her throat was dry; her heart was pounding; she attended the fun; the meals with the Lucassan extended family were directed by her husband with painfully scrupulous care. All the while, her blank eyes appearing insensate to people and things around her.

On the morning of December 28, she woke up at dawn, when it was freezing cold, looked out at the lead-colored clouds covering the top of the mountain. Giang Thanh saw the image of graves. She dared not think further. When she asked Lucassan to take her down the street, to the post office, the conflict that had been simmering for days broke out and could not be concealed.

"What do you call me?"

Giang Thanh looked straight into the eyes of the questioner without hesitation, sharing, "My husband."

"Then you are my wife, the wife I've taken before the Lord. Lucassan felt belittled by the uncompromising gaze of his wife who he thought should have been subject to grateful submission."

"I know, so I do all the work in this house. Not a house but a big castle. I cook what you like."

"That is the job of the housekeeper, the maid, the cook. A wife must satisfy the liking (the want, "*le désir*"–Lucassan adjusted, emphasizing the word) of her husband. But you're a refrigerator. No, it's actually a portable freezer. You look at me and all my family members with porcelain eyes. This is not a one-time incident. But it repeats itself every night, and last Christmas is concrete proof."

Giang Thanh smiled faintly. "You understand that I can't be happy with your family. What they say I don't understand. I'm a Buddhist, and I don't know how to read Christian scriptures. On the day of the church wedding, the priest also sympathized with me. As for the relationship between husband and wife every night, I couldn't satisfy you the way you demanded. I'm an Asian woman. I don't know the "techniques"... And I'm missing my baby. I'm living as though I've died."

Giang Thanh tried to express her thoughts with the scant capacity of French acquired after a month of conjugal life. But because she was an actress, a stage and film director, she was inherently gifted with a delicate accent, so her pronunciation was very accurate.

Lucassan knew he couldn't say more. He clamped down his anger, in the polite manner of a highly cultured Frenchman, and changed into a casual tone: "So what does 'madame' want now?" The word "madame," however, was emphasized to show aloofness, indifference.

"Help me get down the street, to the post office. I need to call my daughter, It's her birthday today."

"I can only help you in the afternoon, after 4 o'clock. I have a lot of work to do after the holidays."

"No, it's too late in the afternoon. The post office would be closed."

"I said, I need to work–don't bother me!"

Giang Thanh turned around and walked out of the room. She growled as she changed into a pair of low-heeled boots. "I don't fucking need anyone!"

She went running down the hill, passing the kilometer post where the road sign read: Clermont - Ferrand, 11 Km. "Even if it is a hundred and one kilometers, I still can get there."

Giang Thanh found the postal worker who had helped her the day before.

"You want to call the daughter. Where's Mr. Lucassan?"

She suppressed her emotions, but they still managed to spill over. "Today is my daughter's birthday. I want to hear her voice. Please help me. I'd be very grateful." She grabbed the postman's hand urgently.

The bell kept ringing, no answer. "You try one more time for me please? Hell, where did she go?!" Giang Thanh lost her composure.

The postal worker was confused and desperate. "Here, here, please help me call this number, also at cité Ho." On the other side of Vietnam, there was the voice of Dau. The voice from hell. The sound. Of the Demon.

"Child's gone! Huh? Where to? Where's the child!?" Giang Thanh dropped the phone and fell face down on the ground.

One year later, Giang Thanh recovered her memory, divorced Lucassan, and moved back to Vietnam. She recalled the cryptographic code and was able to open the bank safe–but all the jewelry, the registration book of the house on Nguyen Trai Street, were all taken, all gone. She also knew the details. On the night of Thanh Giang's birthdate, the cats at the house cried out lamentably. And the neighbors on Lane 222 Nguyen Trai Street saw the girl come out of the house in the evening wearing beautiful clothes, her face as bright as that of an angel. She said to the people she met in the neighborhood, *"I'm going to Uncle D's house to get money from my mother to treat my friends on my birthday."* The girl hadn't come back since that night.

"Then what happened to that old man?" The listener didn't want to spell out the name "D..."

Five years later, also in December, at the end of 2000, the man fell to his death while going to the Golden Stream Lake, Da Lat. From the high hill, he stumbled down into the lake, dying face-down in the water, bruised as if strangled.

The two friends were silent as the car pulled into ABC Market, in Westminster, CA. *"Now do you want me to take you out to eat something?"*

"No, I've called my son to pick me up. How could I eat now!"

Year-end, December 2007.
Written about TTVN

Original PHAN NHAT NAM - Translated KIM VU

About The Author

Born on 9-9-1943 on Hue, Central Vietnam, PHAN NHAT NAM is a soldier, a renowned writer, and a political commentator. A graduate of Da Lat Military Academy, South Vietnam's equivalent of West Point, during the Vietnam War he served for eight years as a soldier in the Red Berets, South Vietnam's elite airborne division, and after that became the country's most prominent war reporter. Following the Communist takeover in 1975, he was imprisoned in Hanoi's infamous "re-education camps" for fourteen years, eight of which being spent in solitary confinement. He was allowed to emigrate to the United States in 1993 under the Orderly Departure Program, and has continued to write and speak about the war and its continuing aftermath, remaining one of the most influential voices in the worldwide overseas Vietnamese community.

His works include (in Vietnamese and English):

- Dấu Binh Lửa: 1969; 1973
- Dọc Đường số 1: 1970
- Ải Trần Gian: 1971
- Dựa Lưng Nỗi Chết: 1972; 1973
- Mùa Hè Đỏ Lửa: 1972; 1973; 1974

- Tù Binh và Hòa Bình: 1974
- Peace & Prisoners of War: 1988
- Những Chuyện Cần Được Kể Lại: 1995
- Đường Trường Xa Xăm: 1995; 1996; 1997
- Đêm Tận Thất Thanh: 1997
- Mùa Đông Giữ Lửa: 1997; 1998.
- A Vietnam War Epilogue: 2013
- Stigmates de Guerre: 2016
- Un Été Embrasé: 2019
- After the War: 2023

Awards:

- War Correspondent Award issued by ARVN Defense Ministry Saigon, South Vietnam, 1972
- National Literature Prize issued by Vietnamese National Resistance Movement, California, USA, 1988

About The Translator

Kim Vu writes poetry, mini stories, essays, translates works from English into Vietnamese and from Vietnamese into English, does color aquarelles.

He has authored more than 20 works, including books of poetry and philosophy in English that are available on Amazon.

www.ingramcontent.com/pod-product-compliance
Lightning Source LLC
LaVergne TN
LVHW092049060526
838201LV00047B/1312